T0098332

ELAINE MORGAN

A Life Behind the Screen

For Kate –
in hope that she is inspired

ELAINE MORGAN
A Life Behind the Screen

DARYL LEEWORTHY

Seren is the book imprint of
Poetry Wales Press Ltd,
Suite 6, 4 Derwen Road, Bridgend, Wales, CF31 1LH

www.serenbooks.com
facebook.com/SerenBooks
Twitter: @SerenBooks

ISBN: 9781781726044
Ebook: 9781781726051

A CIP record for this title is available from the British Library.

The publisher acknowledges the financial assistance
of the Welsh Books Council.

Cover photography: Reach Publishing Services

Printed by Severn, Gloucester.

CONTENTS

FOREWORD

As I was growing up I didn't have to look very far for a role model. Just to the next valley in fact where Elaine Morgan changed the world from her desk in Mountain Ash.

When I was nervous about leaving the Rhondda for Oxford University, someone pointed out there was no need to panic. If Elaine Morgan coped with the culture shock of swapping her Pontypridd school for Lady Margaret Hall in 1939 surely I could manage it in 1987. And that's how I was first inspired by this remarkable Renaissance Woman – though I could only dream of emulating the span of her talents. Elaine's life glittered with achievement. Excelling in science as well as the arts, she created Bafta-winning drama, influenced American feminism and altered the course of evolutionary theory.

Over the years I sought her wisdom many times. As a young journalist in the 1990s I sat with her in front of the fireplace in Mountain Ash to hear the compelling story behind her latest book on Aquatic Ape theory. A decade later we were back in that cosy front room with a film crew for a series on Welsh women's history. Elaine combined anecdote and insight into perfect soundbites, delivered in those gentle Valleys tones.

And for the last ten years of her life we shared column space on *The Western Mail*, the paper that had paid her a guinea for the first story she published as a fiercely bright 11-year-old. What a privilege that was. To be a fellow columnist of Elaine's felt like our local five-a-side team had just signed Lionel Messi. I loved her writing style

– direct, spare, conversational and punchy. That's why her television characters leapt into life from her scripts and her columns left readers feeling they were engaged in a stimulating one-to-one chat. It was also why she could communicate the most complex scientific ideas to the everyday reader.

I also marvelled at the way she took on the chauvinists of evolutionary theory and challenged the scientific establishment. Satisfyingly, those who underestimated the diminutive lady in large spectacles were always the ones left looking small. And I was hugely impressed by her cerebral stamina and agelessness. More than a million people viewed the Ted talk she gave aged 89. She crossed generational boundaries, inspiring the likes of the young American science writer I met who travelled to Wales simply to discover more about her nonagenarian idol.

Yet most of all, I admired the way Elaine stayed true to who she was and where she came from. While this polymath could change intellectual course so deftly, she never altered her identity. As historian Angela John summed up beautifully: "Elaine had roots as well as wings."

Those of us with similar backgrounds have been told by the ignorant and patronising that being a Valley Girl can hold us back. But Elaine said her roots were precisely the reason she succeeded. And she never left them behind. It was so reassuring to hear her underline the values she drew from her upbringing: "Everybody in the valleys thought they were as good as anybody else. They have self-respect that has nothing to do with money and nothing to do with possessions. I was glad to have been brought up that way."

On the night in 2003 when Elaine was awarded the Bafta Cymru Fellowship, Geraint Stanley Jones praised this sense of "unassuming homely brilliance". As the remarkable list of her screenwriting credits rolled – *The Onedin Line, A Testament of*

Youth, The Life and Times of Lloyd George – this was exactly the quality the then 82-year-old icon displayed as she greeted her standing ovation from Wales' broadcasting elite. "I know you're hungry but you must remember this is my first glitzy night out in showbiz for 20 years!" she smiled with her usual down to earth charm.

Though modest and self-effacing, Elaine had immense inner strength. I will never forget the heartbreaking column she wrote in 2011 after the death of her eldest son Dylan from pancreatic cancer. "According to the calendar he was in his sixties but our children are always young to us and it is undoubtedly true that he still had a lot to offer and everything to live for," were her poignant words. Against this backdrop of personal tragedy it would have been understandable if Elaine's take on the world became bleak but her wisdom, humour and positivity continued to shine through every paragraph.

Only illness in the final year of her life ended her weekly missives. Bowing out at the age of 92 she bade farewell with classic Morgan wit: "I haven't really got the hang of retirement yet, but I take it to mean, at least partly, that instead of trying to tell the world how to run itself on more reasonable lines, I will try to do the same for myself. Meanwhile, I enjoy having more leisure time for things like crosswords, Scrabble and watching Bernard Shaw's plays on DVD (with a few chocolates and a glass of sherry) before bed."

As we gathered to say our goodbyes to Elaine when she died in 2013 the global impact she made could be seen in the geographical spread of the tributes. There were messages from Spain, Poland and America while words of homage came from well-known figures ranging from broadcaster Roy Noble to novelist Margaret Drabble.

While it was wonderful to hear Elaine's literary and scientific achievements reiterated, the personal stories from family members resonated even more because they underlined the aspects of her life we weren't so familiar with. We heard she was a great wife, mother and grandmother too.

I was particularly moved by the eulogy given by Elaine's grand-daughter Tan Morgan. She recounted how her Nan believed children's opinions were as important as their elders, illustrating this with the story of a Christmas Day when Mountain Ash was hit by monsoon conditions. Intrigued to hear a relative say "the roads were like rivers", four-year-old Tan wanted an expedition and insisted on seeing the torrents for herself. Elaine took her out into the dark streets and, hand in hand, they waded through the water. "I felt like an explorer," said Tan.

She told more lovely anecdotes of a grandmother who fired her ambitions and intellect as well as her sense of adventure. The command of language Tan displayed in expressing these precious memories showed the spirit of Elaine Morgan lives on in the granddaughter she doted on.

And thanks to this beautifully written and rigorously researched book by Dr Daryl Leeworthy, many more can take inspiration from Elaine Morgan and a legacy that spans both arts and science. Daryl has given Elaine's work the scholarship it deserves and uncovered fascinating biographical detail. In this, her centenary year, there can be no more fitting tribute.

To me, Elaine Morgan remains the ultimate Valleys Girl. My heroine was born there and never really left there but changed the world in between.

Carolyn Hitt, September 2020

INTRODUCTION

Few writers had as profound an influence on the way in which Wales was presented on television, radio, and the stage in post-war Britain as Elaine Morgan. In a career spanning much of the second half of the twentieth century, she penned high-profile adaptations of literary works notably Richard Llewellyn's 1939 novel *How Green Was My Valley* and Vera Brittain's 1933 memoir *Testament of Youth*; biographical serials of David Lloyd George, Gwen John, and Marie Curie; as well as documentaries, dramas, and comedies of her own creation. Put together, her writing 'brought out the flavour of Wales', as the broadcaster and fellow writer Trevor Fishlock observed following Elaine's death, aged 92, in 2013. Like her near contemporaries, Gwyn Thomas, Dylan Thomas, Ron Berry, and fellow Pontypriddian Alun Richards, she endeavoured to show the humanity of her people, but unlike them sought to find a bridge between the two ideas of Wales: the proletarian, Anglophone world of the coalfield into which she was born and the Welsh-speaking world represented by her pre-industrial ancestors, not least (according to family tradition) William Edwards, the eighteenth-century architect responsible for Pontypridd's famous Old Bridge. It was a duality shared with Menna Gallie, the Ystradgynlais-born novelist and translator. A year older than Elaine, Gallie was likewise a socialist and a Welsh speaker. Attributes which made for a different outlook from those male writers who primarily forged the literary traditions of industrial South Wales.[1]

11

This is the first full-length biography of a writer beloved by readers, viewers, and actors, but who has been comparatively neglected, particularly by scholars of Welsh writing, or seen only through the lens of the *Descent of Woman*.[2] So much of Elaine's creative work was released through the ephemeral world of television and radio, and has subsequently been lost in recorded form, even when the scripts she wrote have survived, that such absence was perhaps inevitable. In the words of one critic, 'the work of adaptors ... often tends to be ignored – or worse, taken for granted'.[3] Short stories and poems written as a young woman and published in magazines and journals such as *My Weekly, Homes and Gardens* and the *New Statesman* have long been forgotten, as have several well-regarded plays. Although Elaine hinted in her autobiography at once having started to write a novel, she explained in an interview with the *New Welsh Review* in 1989 that she had little ambition to be a novelist. 'I hear the dialogue and see the people, partly from inside', she explained, 'I don't see weather, clothes, or furniture. That's why I can't write novels. I only write the dialogue'.[4] Such modesty and self-effacement were typical of Elaine, who fostered a public image as the housewife-dramatist, even when in truth this was very far from the reality of her life behind the screen.

Another reason for neglect lies in the absence of a substantial archive of correspondence and manuscripts, which renders exploration of Elaine's private life and the interplay between her domestic and professional existence more difficult than several of her contemporaries. Ron Berry, for instance, left behind diaries and unpublished novels; Gwyn Thomas's archive of correspondence and literary papers is voluminous, as is that of Dylan Thomas and Rhys Davies. Menna Gallie left behind a rich archive of her own, albeit split between the National Library of Wales and Boston University in America. The most substantive collection of Elaine's papers, which are held at Swansea University, comprises the scripts for many of the television programmes with which she was involved – although it is not itself a complete record, even with the addition of papers held at the BBC's Written Archive Centre in Caversham near Reading. Given the extent of Elaine's public engagements, as well as the networks in which she moved, the people with whom she corresponded, and the personal insights provided in her *Western Mail* column, not inconsiderable mitigation of this archival absence is possible. Nevertheless, some of Elaine's personal story, particularly in relation to her creative process and to familial relationships, cannot be fully told – or properly deciphered from the directions and misdirections which she gave to journalists and laid down in her own autobiographical stories.

This is frustrating for the biographer, to be sure, but there is reason enough for persisting with the telling of Elaine Morgan's life, and for restoring to public consciousness the full extent and significance of her quite remarkable career. More than any other Welsh writer of her generation, except perhaps for Alun Richards, who was a decade younger, Elaine made television her medium. This set her apart from Dylan Thomas or Gwyn Thomas, whose most profound broadcast work was (with one or two exceptions in the case of the latter) for radio, but it was also a distinction which set her apart from most of the other screenwriters she worked alongside at the BBC in the 1950s and 1960s, many of whom had initially favoured either the theatre or radio. Donald Wilson, one of the creators of *Doctor Who,* and the producer with whom Elaine enjoyed the closest working relationship at the start of her career, noted this unusual characteristic. Writing in a collection of television plays published in 1960, he argued of Elaine that 'without television and the opportunity it presented, it is doubtful that she would ever have devoted her considerable talents to the writing of drama'. Wilson concluded, 'this makes her work of peculiar interest since it is the product of that comparatively new creative artist, the television playwright who owes loyalty to no other medium'.[5]

Of course, a screenwriting career would have been almost unthinkable had Elaine not been a graduate of Oxford University. Between 1939 and 1942, Elaine read English at Lady Margaret Hall, a period of study made possible by a university exhibition scholarship, a Glamorgan County Council scholarship, and a national miners' welfare scholarship which she was awarded in 1940. Elaine was the first woman from South Wales to receive a mining scholarship to study at Oxford, and one of only three students up to that point. The others were Gwyn Thomas (for French and Spanish) in 1932 and the comparatively unknown Robert Bowen from Aberbeeg (also for English) in 1927.[6] The three were part of a highly selective group of just two hundred students from the coalfields of Britain to be supported in this way between 1927 and 1940, fewer than thirty of whom studied at Oxford or Cambridge. Gwyn and Elaine experienced Oxford in quite different ways, at least insofar as they publicly discussed their time at the university. Gwyn hated St Edmund Hall, finding himself in an environment which was often openly hostile politically, socially, and culturally. Elaine, on the other hand, always claimed to have enjoyed the atmosphere at Lady Margaret Hall and the opportunities which Oxford provided. At worst, Elaine later observed, Oxford seemed to have had an injurious impact on her enthusiasm for writing, but otherwise she loved being there. She explained to the *New Welsh Review* in 1989 that

as a girl, I thought I would be a writer. After three years of studying the great writers at Oxford, I ended up almost totally discouraged. You have to have a great deal of self-confidence to survive an

Oxford literary course and still think you can write. It took ten years to wear off. I think it's a very good training for being a literary critic or a reviewer.

As this book demonstrates, Elaine did have a complicated relationship with Oxford. Whilst her experiences were by no means as bleak as those of Gwyn Thomas, they were not entirely rosy either. The effect of going up from the Rhondda at the height of the Depression was of a different form to going up from Pontypridd at the start of the Second World War, or indeed, as in my own case, in the mid-2000s, but it was nonetheless a shock and forced a period of sharp adjustment.

For Elaine, Oxford provided not only excellent training in the study of English literature, but also a clear opportunity for political expression. She entered the university holding political views mainstream to the Labour politics of her hometown and maintained a careful distance from Communist-led political organisations and their leading members including Iris Murdoch, Denis Healey, and Kingsley Amis. Instead, she joined the Labour-orientated groups whose most prominent figures included future cabinet ministers Roy Jenkins and Tony Crosland. It was after graduating from Oxford and having met her husband Morien Morgan, a former International Brigader from Ynysybwl, that she began to move further to the left, eventually joining the Communist Party whilst living in Burnley in Lancashire. Morien himself had secretly joined the Communist Party as a student at Cardiff, although officially he maintained his links to Labour by serving as chair of the Ynysybwl branch. In later years, although close to communists in the Cynon Valley such as Alistair and Olive Wilson, and recognised by commentators such as the journalist Brinley Evans as having made 'contributions to Celtic nationalism', Elaine re-joined the Labour

Party and rarely discussed her communist period in public.[7] Morien, too, became a prominent member of the Aberdare Labour Party's constituency machine, serving as vice chair in the 1960s.

For many readers, whose image of Elaine Morgan is that of the elderly columnist writing about relatively benign matters, such as figuring out how to fix the 'remote control thingy', or the general experience of being an older person in contemporary Britain, the intervention of radical left-wing politics into the story of her life may well come as a surprise.[8] Yet even at the very end, chronicling the embers of the New Labour government after 2005 and the early days of the Conservative-Liberal Democrat coalition government after 2010, Elaine maintained a sharp political consciousness. She called on the Labour Party, especially, to pull up its socks and to adopt a 'much gutsier manifesto' for future elections lest disillusion and frustration with the political system result in the rise of the 'racialist fringe'.[9] Her comments were in response to the rise of right-wing parties such as the British National Party and the United Kingdom Independence Party. Left-wing politics had always been a feature of Elaine's life. They were part and parcel of her natal milieu and shaped her outlook: from the *Daily Herald* columns she read as a girl, to the activism evident at Oxford university, to her work in the women's movement, the peace movement and anti-Vietnam War protests, and the campaign to end nuclear weapons proliferation after the Second World War.[10]

This was a public commitment to political activity which belied the notion of the housewife-dramatist. Undoubtedly Elaine's politics encouraged her championing of the work of Vera Brittain in the 1970s and the novelist Dorothy Edwards, an ILP supporter and Welsh nationalist, in the 1980s.[11] At various points, Elaine was active in the Fabian Society, the Women's Co-operative Guild, the United Nations Association, and the Campaign for Nuclear Disarmament, as well as the Labour Party and the Communist Party; she taught for the Workers' Educational Association and the National Council of Labour Colleges; she was an influential and active feminist; and she campaigned in favour of devolution and for Welsh-medium education in the South Wales Valleys. The latter aspects of her life and politics set her apart from Alun Richards and Gwyn Thomas, who took the opposite view particularly about constitutional reform, language, and education – but they had been inside the classroom for many years, Elaine had not.[12] In the present age of devolution, such positive views of language and nationhood, as well as advocacy of Welsh medium education, mean that Elaine can be held with a certain degree of reverence whereas, as she observed in her foreword to *The Dark Philosophers* for the Library of Wales series, Gwyn Thomas 'has tended to be lightly air-brushed out of the list of Wales's literary achievers'.[13] Elaine understood the tragedy of that neglect.

In the late twentieth century, particularly amongst an international audience, it was Elaine's scientific work and her feminism which sustained her renown, earning her places at academic conferences, invitations to university campuses including Harvard and University College London, and lucrative paperback publishing contracts with Penguin Books. *The Descent of Woman* (1972), *The Aquatic Ape* (1982), and later works such as *The Descent of the Child* (1994), set out her theories of evolutionary anthropology and helped to popularise the idea that humans had had an aquatic phase in their evolutionary development. Although this idea has continued to be supported or warmly discussed by friends such as Sir David Attenborough, who made a radio documentary series to that effect in 2016, and the American philosopher and academic Daniel Dennett, it has never garnered the enthusiasm of the scientific community and has fallen by the wayside as an explanation for certain human characteristics – including the ability to swim, to hold one's breath underwater, and an appetite for shellfish. Nevertheless, for fifty years, the seemingly universal nature of the aquatic ape theory combined with Elaine's gift for storytelling and argumentation, as well as the vigorous, feminist challenge posed to the 'Tarzanist' theories popular in the 1960s, has proven attractive to a range of lay audiences.

In 1984, for example, the Australian director Tristram Miall, most notable for his work with Baz Luhrmann on the 1992 film *Strictly Ballroom*, made a fifty-minute documentary focusing on Elaine and her work on the aquatic ape theory. Released in 1985, *Water Babies*, the title a nod to Charles Kingsley's satirical, pro-Darwinian children's novel of 1863, brought Elaine's work to life and gave it a sustained awareness in Australia that it might otherwise not have had. Interest maintained more recently by the veteran science broadcaster Robyn Williams, who interviewed Elaine in 2003 for *The Science Show* on Australian radio and provided a sympathetic tribute following her death in 2013. Across the Tasman Sea, Television One in New Zealand drew attention to the same set of ideas apparent in *Water Babies* in an off-beat documentary titled *Hair* (1993). Humorously, Elaine was rung up on a bright yellow novelty telephone to present the case that humans had become the naked ape not because of running around on the savannah, but because of an aquatic phase of evolution. Two decades after that documentary was aired, and forty years after its original publication, Radio New Zealand featured *The Descent of Woman* as part of its Kiwi Summer Reading series in January 2012. The book and the theory have proven survivors.

But there is an unfortunate consequence. For decades, the aquatic ape theory and its scientific controversy have overshadowed the creative and adaptive work for television and radio for which

Elaine deserves greatest credit. It was, after all, the field in which she was genuinely pioneering. Elaine's decision to embrace the novel, creative possibilities of television in the mid-1950s amply justifies her status as one of Wales's greatest talents. Elaine had a global reach, too, with commissions from American and Canadian television in the 1950s as well as a series of broadcast translations of her work for the BBC into European languages such as Dutch and Swedish. Thus, to restore to public consciousness these aspects of Elaine's career, as well as her long forgotten short story writing and poetry, I have focused more fully in this book on what I consider to be her most significant contributions (whilst recognising the undoubted impact of *Descent of Woman* and its sequels). Namely as a dramatist, adult educator, and political campaigner on issues such as Welsh medium education, nuclear disarmament, peace, and the environment and climate change. In shaping this presentation of her life, therefore, I have taken my cue from the British Film Institute's recent promotion of Elaine as a major television dramatist and added my own twist: Elaine Morgan was Wales's most important television writer of the twentieth century.

2020 marks the centenary of Elaine's birth in Pontypridd. The world she grew up in has now long gone; as are the mines in which her father and grandfathers worked, to say nothing of her father-in-law John E. Morgan of Ynysybwl. In her lifetime, she was awarded an honorary doctorate, an OBE, a range of awards for television writing including the prestigious Prix Italia, honorary fellowship of several universities including Swansea and Cardiff, and had buildings named after her – not least at Glyntaff in the shadow of the former Pontypridd Intermediate School for Girls where she studied and, for a brief time, taught. Since her death a few months shy of her 93rd birthday, Elaine has been accorded a blue plaque (erected by the Rhys Davies Trust in Pontypridd

Library, where she wrote her first short stories as a child), and in 2019 was one of a shortlist of five in a public competition to choose the first statue of a woman to be erected in Wales. Her life is now also the subject of permanent exhibitions at Pontypridd Museum and Mountain Ash Public Library, the latter a building central to her career as a science writer. This is the story of how all that came about: how Elaine Morgan developed, through her work for radio, television and the stage, a public image of Wales infused with the politics, history, and culture of the South Wales Coalfield, her birth-place and her life-long home, but one always conscious of its changing nature.

ONE
BILLY'S KID

Elaine Morgan was born on 7 November 1920 in Hopkinstown, a mining community set along the road and railway linking the Rhondda to Pontypridd. With her parents and one set of grandparents, she grew up in a 'dilapidated and bug-ridden' terraced house typical of the South Wales Coalfield: 54 Telelkebir Road.[1] The family was poor – Elaine's father, Billy, a pumpsman at the Great Western Colliery, spent almost a decade on the dole – and 'lived all the time in the kitchen because we could only afford to have a fire in one room'.[2] In the relative classlessness of the coalfield, however, Elaine did not feel deprived: with two dole packets coming in – the other from her grandfather, Fred – and only one child to support, Elaine's family were able to survive. An allotment at Coedpenmaen on the other side of town provided additional food, and Billy turned his hand to odd jobs to bring in money or favours in kind. It was at grammar school where Elaine encountered less subtle differences in social status and where she was made more aware of poverty and the distinctions of class. 'There were', she recalled later, 'only four from the Rhondda ward in form 2a', the other pupils in her year came from the more affluent parts of the town.

The Rhondda ward separated Pontypridd from the famous Rhondda valleys and included the mining communities to the northwest of the town centre: Hopkinstown, Maesycoed, Pwll-gwaun, and Trehafod. In later years, by then already resident in the Cynon valley, Elaine staked a tongue-in-cheek claim to be from the Rhondda because of her childhood in Hopkinstown. The *Western Mail*, which was not overly enthusiastic about the idea, observed that this was a 'rather precarious right'.[3] For those looking in from the outside, such designations of place can seem trifling: a hyper-localism which matters very little compared with the more obvious differences between the valleys and the wider world, but for residents they are serious. And are felt by those absorbed in them, then and now. The novelist, screenwriter, and playwright, Alun Richards, who grew up a short distance away from Elaine, but in the decidedly more affluent Graigwen district of Pontypridd, recalled that 'although my grandmother would never admit to it, we actually lived on the extreme tip of the Rhondda Valley'.[4] Like-wise, Gwyn Thomas, who really was from the Rhondda, regarded Pontypridd as the 'hub of sophistication. It was an older, more stylish place'. He continued:

> As an ancient market town it had an assurance of roots that gave its life an altogether more dignified pulse than one could feel in the scattered townships that lay between Porth and Maerdy, Trealaw and Treherbert.[5]

The iconic Old Bridge completed in 1756 had drawn tourists to the river Taff, including the artist JMW Turner, almost a century before the Rhondda valleys burst into life. Indeed, for every resident of the Rhondda in 1851, there were at least five living in the town of Pontypridd.

One of the clearest distinctions between the valley and the town opened in 1921: Pontypridd's branch of Woolworth's.[6] At the time, there were only half a dozen branches in the whole of Wales and only one other in the valleys – at Aberdare, which opened in 1919. The earliest branch to open in the Rhondda followed in 1923, at Penygraig. The importance of Woolworth's was drawn by Gwyn Thomas, who wrote – with tongue only partly in cheek – that

> The day on which the Pontypridd branch of the Woolworth chain was unveiled was one of the brightest of my life. I had decided that I would be the first through the door of the new transatlantic temple… When the Woolworth's doors opened I was the second in. I had been stunned by a bullying woman with an umbrella who, on a flawless day, wanted to use it on something other than rain, but only briefly. The first thing that caught my eye were blue fruit-salad dishes at a penny each. The colour fascinated me. It had the same shade of ultra-marine as the whole of that serene morning. On top of that, fruit salad at the time was an exotic touch. People still asked for the official permit of the chapel before laying lip to pagan tit-bits as sliced peaches and pineapple-chunks.[7]

Alun Richards's ancestors, of course, had been part of the pre-industrial farming community of upland Glamorgan and had a pronounced antipathy to the denizens of the coal rush which transformed the Rhondda and Pontypridd in the second half of the nineteenth century. His grandparents, with whom he lived as a child, were shopkeepers whose nervous reaction to the arrival of Woolworth's is easy to imagine. Elaine's family, on the other hand, had joined the coal rush, coming from the South West of England to work in (and around) the mining industry. They arrived in Pontypridd just as the town entered its golden age, growing from a population of around twenty thousand in 1891 to almost fifty thousand a generation later – eighty percent of the workforce was employed by the coal mines.[8] Almost every building of note, with the exception of the lido, was erected in this period: from the public library which opened in 1890, to the municipal buildings designed by London-based architect Henry Hoare and opened in 1906, to the YMCA of 1910, the cottage hospital of 1912, and the court-house of 1913. An Edwardian flourish of construction which continues to define much of the town's overarching architectural character.

Elaine's father's family, the Floyds, came from the Cornish village of Gwinear, halfway between Penzance and Redruth. Although small and quaint in the twenty-first century, Gwinear benefitted from the early nineteenth century boom in the Cornish metal mining industries and nearly doubled in size from just over sixteen hundred people in 1801 to three thousand forty years later. At the heart of industrial Gwinear was the Herland mine with its rich deposits of tin, copper, zinc and silver. Although worked since the early eighteenth century, the introduction of steam engines designed and manufactured by Matthew Boulton and James Watt and, later, by Richard Trevithick, led not only to greater prosperity and productivity but also created the specialist skill of the mechanical engineer. Men such as Israel Floyd, Elaine's great-great grandfather. Born in Gwinear in 1798, Israel Floyd spent his working life fixing and repairing steam engines. He died in Cornwall in 1856. His son, Israel, born in 1824, followed in his footsteps and trained as a mechanic, beginning his career in Cornwall before moving to South Wales in the 1860s – just as Cornish industry entered terminal decline. By the start of the next decade, he was living with his wife, Eleanor, and their family, in Cefn in the Rhymney valley, and working for Messrs Powell and Co variously as a mechanical engineer or colliery mechanic.[9] By 1881, the family had moved to Pontypridd.

The youngest Israel Floyd, Elaine's grandfather, broke with tradition and became (for a time) a colliery engine driver rather than a mechanic. He, too, had been born in Cornwall but lived most of his life in South Wales – remaining in Pontypridd even after his parents had moved on to Bedwas, near Caerphilly.[10] In an effort to escape the mines, and with a spirit of entrepreneurial aspiration and (perhaps) bourgeois pretension, Israel established a boot and shoe repair shop at his home in Trehafod Road, Hopkinstown. Unfortunately, he was not a particularly successful businessman and faced bankruptcy in 1892 – he returned to work as an engine fitter at the colliery. Catherine, Elaine's grandmother, re-established the shop in her name and ran it more successfully until 1902, when it finally closed.[11] Catherine, née Edwards, came from the village of Llanfabon situated five miles to the north-east of Pontypridd. According to the story told within the family it was Catherine who was related to William Edwards, the venerable builder of the Old Bridge and minister at the Methodist chapel in Groeswen, on the hillside above Caerphilly. Whether true, or not, such links were made and told with considerable pride – a reflection of the migrant family's desire to establish historic roots in their new community.

In the years which followed the bankruptcy of Israel and Catherine Floyd's shop, an air of tragedy lingered. Israel, the fourth of his name in the family line, and the eldest son of Israel and Catherine, died suddenly aged fourteen in 1894. A few years later, in 1900, the family's eldest child, Margaret Ann, died after complications in childbirth. Her young son, Israel Wootten, came to live with his grandparents. As Elaine put it in her memoir, Catherine 'was presented with the newborn of her eldest daughter and brought him up too as her own'. That was not the end of the family's misfortune. The baby Israel died aged just two, in 1902. His father, Paul, a colliery timberman, remarried in 1904 and eventually moved away to work in Carmarthenshire. Then, in the summer of 1905, Israel and Catherine's youngest son, Israel Garfield, was hit by a train near the Great Western Colliery in Hopkinstown.[12] He was ten years old. According to the newspaper accounts of the accident, the young boy's legs were broken in the impact. Elaine told a different version, which was surely much closer to the truth: 'both his legs [were] cut off and [he] died before they could carry him home'.

The Floyds did not only know sadness, of course. Elaine's aunt, Eunice, was an accomplished musician and studied piano in the 1890s with local teacher and conductor T.D. Edwards. In 1899, after winning a scholarship based on her performance in the entrance examinations, she became the first member of the family to proceed to secondary school entering the girls department of the county school (the division between boys' and girls' schools had not yet formalised).[13] With an education and qualifications in music, Eunice might have been destined for a career as a teacher – the commonest vocational means of social mobility for working-class women in that period. But no: in the spring of 1912, Eunice married a local collier, David Idris Williams, and settled down. Eunice's encouragement in education was not unusual for Floyd women. On Catherine's insistence, each of the sisters (Margaret and Eunice) had been taught dressmaking skills to 'keep them respectably independent whatever happened'. There was no such educational opportunity for Billy Floyd, the surviving younger son: Elaine's father. Born in 1891, he left school aged fourteen in 1905 and started work at the Great Western Colliery as a striker with the colliery blacksmith – the job he kept for almost ten years until the outbreak of the First World War.

Olive Neville, Elaine's mother, also came from an English family. Olive's father, Frederick, was born in the village of East Coker, near Yeovil, in 1869. His parents, William and Mary, were agricultural labourers – as their ancestors had been for generations. Like countless young men of his generation, Frederick escaped life on the farms of Somerset when he migrated to Pontypridd and began working in the mining industry. Olive's mother, Martha, likewise came from East Coker and before marrying Fred had worked for several years as a domestic servant to the local gentry. According to the stories passed down to Elaine, Fred and Martha had a difficult marriage. He was, in Elaine's view, a 'scallywag poacher who gambled and drank'; whereas Martha had 'acquired ideas above her station'. It was this domestic difficulty which caused Olive's childhood to be rather more peripatetic than Billy Floyd's had been, although there were undoubted similarities. Fred and Martha lived in a state of constant economic flux, moving frequently from house to house in and around Pontypridd – and, for a time, back home to Somerset – in search of a stable financial footing. As Elaine later explained, Fred 'found labouring jobs on the surface, navvying and road mending, and even an entrepreneurial venture to do with a fish and chip cart, but nothing prospered'.

In fact, the fish and chip cart made the pages of the local newspapers in 1907 when it was involved in a dispute between Elaine's grandparents and their former lodger, Geronza Curatti, an Italian immigrant and colleague of Fred's at the colliery. Curatti had encouraged Fred and Martha to establish their fish and chip business, but promptly sued them for more than five pounds which the Italian claimed was unpaid from the 'deal' they had originally struck. Martha, in turn, sued Curatti for the same amount, which she held to be adequate compensation for 'peeling potatoes ... by hand at the rate of from 5cwt to 7cwt per week relinquishing all other occupation and amusement in the endeavour'. She also insisted that Curatti pay for his Christmas dinner since 'she would not like to provide food for a Christmas dinner ... at less than 7s 6d'. The remark – an indication, perhaps, of the snobbish air which Martha cultivated – caused general laughter in the courtroom. The Italian won the case but agreed, magnanimously, to pay for his dinner.[14] Curatti went on to use the proceeds of the court case to establish himself in the ice cream trade but got into more serious trouble in 1920 when he was charged with the attempted murder of the manager of Pontypridd Ice Works.[15]

Elaine's parents first met in about 1908, when Olive was about fourteen and Billy almost seventeen, but they did not marry until the spring of 1919. Their courtship was elongated partly by the age gap, although that was hardly unusual, by Billy's war service, and by the watchful eye which Martha kept on her daughter's behaviour. After a serious, almost fatal illness, at the beginning of the twentieth century, Martha eschewed domestic labour leaving much of the cooking and cleaning to Olive. The demands grew ever greater after the religious revival of 1904-5, during which Martha was 'saved', with Olive taking on the entire burden of keeping the Neville household going. Elaine takes up the story: 'A message was sent to the school saying that Olive Neville's education must be considered at an end, as her mother was a permanent invalid and her services were indispensable at home'. One solitary dispensation which Martha made to on-going education for Olive was to allow her daughter to sit in on the dressmaking lessons being taught to the Floyd sisters across the road. Of course, it was soon their brother who caught Olive's attention rather than the essentials of making and repairing clothes, and the hillsides rather than the Floyd family kitchen which provided respite from home.

The idyll was broken by the outbreak of the First World War in 1914. Billy volunteered almost immediately, serving as an orderly with the British Red Cross and the St John Ambulance.[16] Olive, too, became active as a fundraiser in the Rhondda ward for wartime charities.[17] For the first few months he was in France, Billy kept a diary recording his day-to-day experiences at the base hospitals in

Nantes and Rouen where he worked.[18] He captured some of the tensions evident between the Royal Army Medical Corps and the Voluntary Aid Detachments staffed by the Red Cross and the St John Ambulance, as well as his own approach to the war. In one entry, he described, in vivid detail, the injuries to a soldier and his own anxiety when treating the man.

> His mouth was wide open couldn't shut it and looking down into his mouth could see all black inside with all teeth blown out on side and front, and several other side all loose. Could be pushed away. Shake when wiping mouth clean with lint and cotton wool. I have had to give him drink all night through little glass, shout to let him know its coming and pour drop in. He can't see as all the face is swollen up black so much so as to close his eyes up. Got awful job to understand him when talking with mouth wide open. Can understand some things if you say what to him once or twice he'll start to say *O Christ, Jesus Christ Almighty* + heaps of other pretty things. Man with bullet in skull very quiet not a sound from him would not be surprised to walk over+ find him dead.[19]

The diary shows Billy Floyd to have been witty and genial, very much the practical joker described by Elaine in her memoir, but with the evident weakness of having only had an elementary education. Towards the end of the war, Billy transferred to the Royal Field Artillery and gained a very different perspective from that of the hospitals far from the front lines. Billy proved himself to be an able soldier, as well as an observant and enterprising medical orderly, and served for much of 1919 in Germany in the British army of occupation. It was whilst Billy was on leave early in that year that he and Olive married; he eventually returned home to Pontypridd at the beginning of 1920 after almost five and a half years away.

The army taught Billy new skills and he moved into a different role at the colliery on resuming work there – a pumpsman. It was now his job to operate the underground pumping equipment and the great fans which circulated air and to ensure that both worked. A better salary meant that Billy and Olive could afford a house of their own: 54 Telelkebir Road, Hopkinstown. But repairs, buying furniture, and keeping up with the mortgage left them with little money and so to make ends meet, Olive's mother and father, Martha and Fred, moved in 'bringing their furniture and halving the burden of basic costs'. Billy's parents, Israel and Catherine, lived a short distance away in Oliver Street.[20] Multigenerational living was a short-term solution which became a long-term arrangement, bequeathing to Elaine a childhood surrounded by four very different adults.[21] There was the vigorous Baptist faith of Elaine's grandmother, Martha, who was no more willing to undertake domestic chores than she had been in her own house, and the caddish opportunism of her grandfather, Fred. There was the down-to-earth practicality of Olive and the have-a-go optimism of Billy. Elaine's father was also responsible for infusing the politics of the Soiuth Wales Miners' Federation and the Labour Party into the family dynamic.

This was unavoidable in the coalfield of the 1920s. Six months after Elaine was born, the mining industry was brought to a standstill by the first national coal dispute in almost ten years – a harbinger of the far more tumultuous events of 1926. As a loyal member of the South Wales Miners' Federation, Billy was involved in both. Central to the disputes was the decline in the export market for steam coal and pressure from the coal combines and their shareholders to reduce wages to compensate for diminishing profits. As Britain's largest export coalfield, the struggle was acute in South Wales – tens of thousands of miners lost their jobs, tens of thousands left the coalfield to find work elsewhere, the Edwardian largesse which had been a feature of Billy and Olive's childhood seemed increasingly remote. At nearby Capel Rhondda, the local minister, Robert Gwenffrwd Hughes, earned the scorn of some of the chapel deacons when he opened a soup kitchen in the chapel vestry in 1926 to support the struggling members of the congregation. The deacons felt the chapel should have stood apart from the dispute, recalled Rev. Hughes's son, Alun, and remained a neutral pillar of the community. They were quickly reminded of the parable of the fishes and the loaves.[22]

Although Elaine later insisted that it was her experiences at Oxford University which gave her a political awareness, there can be little doubt that she was at least partially absorbed in the concerns of the Left by the reading material to which she had access at home or in the public library. As a child she entered and won competitions for writing and art which appeared in the *Daily Herald*, the Labour-supporting national newspaper common to the reading habits of many in the South Wales Valleys, including Billy Floyd. One such prize, of half a crown, was won in September 1932 as part of the Bobby Bear Club's 'pocket money' challenge; a second followed in 1933 when Elaine was awarded an Ensign pocket camera for her artistic talents.[23] Launched in 1930, the Bobby Bear Club was one of several newspaper clubs targeted at children in the 1920s and 1930s, and issued membership badges and certificates, handbooks, and illustrated annuals, all under the genial 'leadership' of Aunt Kitsie.[24] With its motto – Make Friends – and sense of camaraderie, it is not difficult to appreciate why an only child such as Elaine would enjoy being part of the club.[25]

The Bobby Bear Club competitions were not the only creative outlet for Elaine. Aged eleven, she sold her first short story – *Kitty in Blunderland* – to the *Western Mail* for a guinea. It was published in the paper's weekly edition, the *Cardiff Times,* on 30 September 1932. The story began with the following lines:

It was the end of the most wonderful day in Kitty's life and she was lying on her back on the pile of sweet-smelling hay on Uncle Bob's hay cart. She had spent a whole week at the farm.[26]

Kitty in Blunderland reflected an absorption in a range of children's literature. Elaine explained to the newspaper reporter who came to interview her that her favourite writers included Charles Dickens and Robert Louis Stevenson, both of whom can be detected in the story's narrative structure. Beatrix Potter was an undoubted influence as well. Pontypridd Library, the heart of the town's literary culture, was a fundamental part of Elaine's life and she spent hours reading her way through the books on the shelves. This literary immersion enabled Elaine to write poetry, accomplished enough to win prizes at the school eisteddfod, and publishable essays. Indeed, it was as an essayist that she next appeared in the *Western Mail* when her study of the National Museum in Cardiff was selected as one of the winners in the annual St David's Day competition in 1934.[27] The piece underlined one of the themes consistent to Elaine's life: her belief in Welsh nationhood and the need for its history and sense of self to be told to the wider world.

They were sentiments which she shared with the novelist Dorothy Edwards (1902-1934), to whom Elaine was drawn as an adult. Born in Ogmore Vale, Edwards was an ardent socialist but moved towards the ideas of Welsh nationalism through her association with Saunders Lewis. After a flourishing literary career in the 1920s, Edwards fell into a deep depression in the early 1930s and took her own life in January 1934 by jumping off a railway bridge near Caerphilly. She was cremated at the municipal crematorium at Glyntaff, within touching distance of Elaine's secondary school. Half a century later, Elaine drew on this sense of fellowship in her introductions to Virago's reissue of Dorothy Edwards's writings: *Rhapsody* (1927) and *Winter Sonata* (1928). Both versions of the introduction established Elaine's obvious sympathy with the 'brave causes' at the heart of Dorothy Edwards's worldview – socialism and Welsh nationalism – and underscored the provincialism which both shared, knowingly and unknowingly, and to some extent accepted. Although Elaine was never seriously tempted politically by the Welsh nationalist party, Plaid Cymru, throughout her life she expressed her support for the Welsh language, Welsh medium education, devolution, and for nationhood, and was seen as having 'tremendous influence in propagating the unique claims of the Welsh.[28] The 1934 essay was the earliest published expression of those ideas. She wrote:

> There is no more tragic picture in the annals of world history than a small country which, having been conquered by a stronger neighbour, sees all its art, traditions, language, commerce, in fact, all of it in any way emblematic of a separate national spirit being gradually merged into those of the other people. So, any event which helped to prevent this catastrophe would stand out in the minds of the people as one of the greatest episodes in the history of the country.
>
> On March 19, 1907, occurred such a victory for Wales. The building of a National Museum of Wales had been discussed in Parliament a few years before; a clause in the National Institutions Bill had enabled the National Council to establish it and on that day was granted the Royal Charter of incorporation.
>
> The success of the scheme was owing largely to the perseverance and untiring efforts of Lord Pontypridd – the first president of the Museum – William Jones and Herbert Lewis. The actual building did not begin until 1911, and because of the Great War it was not until 1927 that it was completed and opened by King George V, but the granting of the Charter prepared for the estab-

lishment of the greatest educational and national institution in Wales.

Apart from a few comparative collections from England and Europe, all the exhibits – geology, botany, art, zoology, archaeology, science, sculpture – are all Welsh, and a considerable portion is devoted to welsh industry and the lives of the people in olden days. Although the Museum is not yet complete and open to the public, it truly fulfils the purpose for which it was build, 'To teach the world about Wales and the Welsh people about their own fatherland'.

These sentiments were encouraged by the nurturing learning environment which Elaine enjoyed at Pontypridd Intermediate School for Girls, where she began studying in 1932. Set on the hillside at Glyntaff and overlooking the busy community of Treforest, the striking red brick school building was a beacon for the girls, mainly from Pontypridd's more well-to-do districts, who won places to study there. Elaine described the buildings in her column in the *Western Mail* in 2010. Modest classrooms with desks, blackboards and chalk, tiled walls and round windows, and the parquet flooring made of intricate blocks of polished wood. To preserve the character of the floor, the headmistress, Miss Bedford[29], insisted that her pupils 'remove our outdoor shoes, hang them in shoe-bags in the cloakroom, and change into "ward shoes"'.[30] Life at grammar school suited Elaine, and she thrived in most of her classes – particularly in the sciences and languages. In contrast with the economic bleakness of the 1930s, Elaine painted her school days in vibrant hues:

> In the summer on the extensive lawns we sometimes performed dances in flowing draperies, like nymphs on a Grecian urn. Normally we wore gymslips and the old school tie, and outdoors had to wear detested school caps of an unbecoming pudding-basin shape with yellow stripes. We were very well taught. There was

plenty of music, and exciting annual highlights like the school play and the Eisteddfod. I was very happy there.[31]

In 1937, she passed her Central Welsh Board examinations. As was then common, her name was published in the pages of the *Western Mail* to record her achievement.[32] In the lower forms, Elaine had focused her efforts on the sciences completing her standard school certificate in chemistry, physics and biology, together with Latin and Welsh. For various reasons, not least the possibility of winning a scholarship to study at university more easily in the arts compared with the sciences, together with her relative successes in poetry and short story writing, and voracious reading habits, she opted to focus on English in the Sixth Form. She thrived, absorbing the plays of George Bernard Shaw, William Shakespeare, and a range of literature most adults in the town had yet to tackle. She won the school's English prize and was chosen to serve as Head Girl.[33] When the results of the higher school certificate were published in August 1939, Elaine's name was top of the list.[34]

At some point in Elaine's final year in Sixth Form, the decision was made to try for Oxford University. No pupil had ever won a place to study there, but the headmistress, Mary Jenkins, who had replaced Catherine Bedford in 1935, encouraged the application perhaps with one eye on achieving that which her predecessors had not. In her later telling, with typical modesty, Elaine suggested that the process was rather like that of a 'promising horse ... entered for the Grand National, without consulting the horse'. To matriculate, Elaine was required to supplement her Welsh and Latin with a modern foreign language: she chose French. Jenkins, a languages teacher by training, provided material support for Elaine's efforts to 'mug up' in her new subject (and prepare for the supplementary examination[35]), and undertook much of the research into college choices and the application process. It was Jenkins who narrowed the selection to Lady Margaret Hall, the senior (and avowedly Anglican) women's college founded in Oxford in 1878, although the more liberal and non-denominational Somerville College or St Hugh's College, with its emphasis on providing an Oxford education for the poorest, would seem more obvious choices to have made.

Elaine was interviewed at Lady Margaret Hall by the college principal, the economist Lynda Grier (1880-1967).[36] Profoundly deaf as a child, Grier earned a reputation as a listener whose character displayed detachment and reasoned and balanced judgement.[37] Of the occasion, Elaine remembered relatively little save the long walk from the door to where Grier was sitting, the speed with which the interview was completed, and the enthusiasm displayed by the principal for Elaine's proficiency in Latin. 'I suppose it was quite an Oxfordish thing to be good at', Elaine reflected years later. But it was also a very Elaine-ish thing to be a good at: she had a demonstrable enthusiasm for etymology and the linguistic development of the English language, skills which no doubt played a part in her winning a place at Oxford. In the spring of 1939, a letter arrived to that effect: she was to commence in September, at the start of Michaelmas term.[38] With a county scholarship, an exhibition scholarship from Lady Margaret Hall, and eventually a scholarship from the Miners' Welfare Fund, Elaine was able to live in Oxford with relative ease – certainly in comparison to the previous person from the South Wales Coalfield to win such a scholarship: the novelist Gwyn Thomas.

Elaine's experience was different in almost every way to Gwyn's, not merely because of money: he grew to hate the university and the people who surrounded him at St Edmund Hall, and was often lonely, whereas Elaine fell in love both with Oxford and with a fellow undergraduate. Gwyn experienced a very deep and serious depression and penurious hardship, committing his ideas to paper in private or in correspondence with members of his family, Elaine found outlets for her increasing political awareness and literary creativity in more public arenas. Perhaps because 'I'd entered the place trying to equip myself with mental armour of stoical indifference in case I couldn't cope', Elaine adapted relatively well to Oxford life. But equally, as an only child, Elaine was used to being alone and to being absorbed in her own thoughts. She found company at Oxford in the same manner as at school in Pontypridd. Gwyn, on the other hand, as the youngest child in a family of twelve, had travelled in the opposite direction, going from the nurturing – if competitive – environment of the Rhondda to a socially and culturally isolating cloister. Nor was Pontypridd in 1939, which had begun to recover from the quagmire of the Depression, quite the same as the Rhondda of 1931.

Winning a place at Oxford was a tremendous achievement, particularly as the first girl from a Pontypridd school. In her later life, Elaine played down that success, focusing instead on the apparent clash of cultures which accompanied her first journey to Lady Margaret Hall at the age of eighteen. She told the story of her encounter with a young mother and a pram whom she met not far from Carfax – the church at the centre of Oxford. The mother had offered to store Elaine's suitcase in the pram for the long walk out to Norham Gardens in north Oxford, where the college was located. Picking out a Welsh accent, the mother asked Elaine why she had come to Oxford. Elaine explained she was going to Lady Margaret Hall for an interview, without clarifying that she meant an interview for a place to study. The mother wished Elaine well, 'it would be a walkover. They were glad to get hold of anybody these days ... owing to the number of girls going off to work in factories, where the money was better'. For all that it provided a wry anecdote, this was hardly an unusual conversation. In fact, almost every young woman who left the South Wales Valleys in search of work, particularly from the Rhondda and Pontypridd, found employment in domestic service.[39]

In different circumstances, Elaine might have joined their ranks becoming a maid or a cook in a college, or in a senior don's private household, rather than a student. But through a combination of intellectual nurture at school and her own remarkable academic prowess, she proved herself a unique kind of South Walian migrant: one destined to escape a lifetime of enforced politeness in the face of privilege and wealth. More than two decades hence, in March 1963, at the prize day to mark the fiftieth anniversary of Pontypridd Intermediate School for Girls – by then, Pontypridd Girls' Grammar School – Elaine spoke about her experiences of going up to Oxford University. She talked warmly of the 'flying start' given to her by her teachers, some of which had been fictionalised in her recent television series *A Matter of Degree* (1960), and encouraged the young women in the audience to cherish their schooldays, 'for all the knowledge acquired in school would come in useful later on'.[40] Perhaps, even for just a moment, Elaine recalled in her own mind the encouragements of Miss Jenkins and others given before making that first journey in 1939.

TWO
A MATTER OF DEGREE

Elaine went off to university shortly after the outbreak of the Second World War. 'I had', she recalled later, 'moved into a kind of dream world'.[1] The city was more silent than usual, since the church bells would peal only in the event of an invasion, and the autumnal colours were beginning to set in. After acquiring the accoutrements of undergraduate life, such as a gown and a bicycle, she began to settle into the world of formal hall (that is, a three-course evening dinner), servants and cleaners called scouts, and 'nothing but deep silence and the occasional owl'. For several months she felt like a stowaway, uncertain of whether she truly belonged in Oxford at all. Such feelings were amplified by the situation at home, where Billy Floyd was dying of heart disease and even walking short distances had become a great challenge for him. In the confusion of the phoney war and the blackout, Elaine's mother, Olive, had to race around Pontypridd searching for a doctor who could provide an oxygen cylinder to ease Billy's breathing difficulties and provide a modicum of palliative care. Billy died shortly before Christmas, 1939, aged forty-eight.[2] Elaine was just nineteen and utterly devastated by the loss of her father to whom she was devoted.

In another household, Elaine might well have been asked to come home, to find a job, and to support the household financially. Having delayed her first term exams to attend the funeral, such a decision could have been made without serious repercussion. But 'chucking it in was the last thing I wanted' and it was the last thing Olive wished for her daughter; and so 54 Telelkebir Road became lodgings for rookie officers from the nearby police station whilst Elaine continued with her studies at Oxford. In contrast to life in Pontypridd, daily routine at Lady Margaret Hall in the autumn of 1939 showed little sign of having altered from the interwar years, apart from the quiet, with the city's calendar set by the routine of the university. This changed during the course of the academic year, however, and by the summer of 1940 Oxford had become 'a maelstrom of civil servants and London officials' and 'sandbags cluttered the streets and buildings'.[3] Similarly, the call up of male undergraduates from the other colleges into the armed forces meant that women – who had only been admitted to full degrees in 1920 and were in residence in women's colleges, themselves at a remove from the city centre – gained increased prominence in the student population.

Lady Margaret Hall itself, along with Somerville, St Hugh's, St Anne's, and St Hilda's, experienced several distinct changes as a result of wartime conditions, particularly after the fall of France. Firstly, there was the complexion of the non-teaching staff, which became older and fewer as the lure of a munitions job reduced the number of younger scouts and dining room waitresses. Secondly, there was the turning over of the college gardens and open spaces to allotments as part of the Dig for Victory campaign: the undergraduates were expected to volunteer some of their time to the war effort – a minimum of six hours a week. Although as Elaine reflected later, 'by and large the students did not come from the horny-handed classes, and the response was poor. They were gently prodded in the right direction by two successive dinners featuring boiled rice as a vegetable followed by rice pudding as a dessert'.

Other tasks included ambulance driving, nursing, administering first aid, child welfare, fire watching and acting as air raid wardens. Elaine, who was used to the family allotment at home, and was one of the more experienced gardeners, readily assisted in the growing of potatoes.

Outside college, Elaine found herself immersed in the turbulent left-wing politics of the university in the early stages of the war. Whilst it was not the case that her participation in student politics began her politicisation, she was already an enthusiastic reader of the *Daily Herald* and could hardly have evaded the political ethos of Pontypridd in the 1930s, it did provide an opportunity to participate in the organisation of political activity. Oxford also brought her into direct contact with future Labour ministers such as Roy Jenkins, Tony Crosland, Denis Healey, and Edmund Dell, with the future novelists Iris Murdoch and Kingsley Amis, and with the poets Philip Larkin and John Heath-Stubbs. Distracted by events at home, Elaine was not as active in the Oxford University Labour Club (OULC) in her first term as she was to become later on; however, she would have had to be very divorced from any political activity at the university to have avoided the tensions which eventually split the Labour Club. The crux was which side of the debate on the conduct of the war the members fell: the anti-war Communist Party line or the pro-war Labour Party line, which repudiated it.[4]

The debate came to its conclusion on 24 April 1940, when nearly three hundred members voted – symbolically – on whether to follow the national Labour Party's disaffiliation of the University Labour Federation (ULF). The latter had fallen under the influence of the Communist Party and come out in favour of making peace with Germany. One hundred and eighty students voted to maintain the OULC's affiliation to the ULF, one hundred and eight against. 'In consequence', recorded one newspaper, 'the supporters of disaffiliation are leaving the club and forming a new Social Democrat organisation'.[5] Roy Jenkins and Tony Crosland resigned immediately from the OULC executive and the club's president, G.D.H. Cole, followed suit.[6] A week later, Herbert Morrison appeared in Oxford to help launch the Oxford University Democratic Socialist Club (OUDSC). During his speech, Morrison thundered that the 'so called communists' are nothing more than Nazi apologists. The *Daily Herald* recorded Morrison as saying that

> because of reactionary so-called Communist influences there had been among certain numbers of young people too much syndicated imported politics, too many syndicated doubtful resolutions and too many syndicated slogans. This kind of thing was Fascist rather than Socialist in its mentality, and perhaps it explains the reason why our so-called Communists have more or less become apologists for the Nazis. It is a sad business but it shows the danger of a political party, as well as the individual, forfeiting intellectual integrity and independence of judgement.[7]

The democratic socialists grew rapidly in number, with more than three hundred paid up by the end of Trinity term, 1940, and branches across most of the colleges in Oxford.[8] They carried a membership card noting that the club stood for a 'a policy of Democratic Socialism. It associates itself with the struggle of the Labour Party and the Trade Union movement to win Socialism by democratic methods.' Tony Crosland served as the OUDSC's founding chairman. Elaine remembered him as being 'tall, handsome, charismatic, with romantic hair and a mellifluous voice'. Roy Jenkins, the club's leading figure, served initially as treasurer, with Ian Durham, a mature undergraduate, taking on the role of secretary. The agenda for that first term involved speakers, in addition to Herbert Morrison, such as Richard Crossman, Hugh Dalton, and the academic Bjarne Braatov whose study of Swedish social democracy had been published the previous year. [9] Elaine joined the executive committee of the OUDSC during Trinity term, 1941, at the end of her second year at Oxford, having spent the previous term as the club's college organiser at Lady Margaret Hall.[10] In March 1941, she was also elected to the post of assistant editor of the club's bulletin, the *Oxford Socialist* – a role she maintained through until the end of the academic year. [11]

As a result, was Elaine propelled to the forefront of Oxford's student politics. Over Easter 1941, she was tasked with undertaking a commission (that is, a research project) on the family allowance to inform both the club's subsequent activities and to add to the Labour Party's own research on the topic ahead of a post-war general election.[12] Elaine's work came a full eighteen months before the release of the Beveridge Report, published in December 1942, which contained its own proposals for the introduction of a family allowance. Roy Jenkins undertook a similar commission on transport. Returning to university at the start of Trinity term, Elaine reported her findings, and gained a new task – to speak as the club's designated 'paper speaker' in a joint-debate with the Oxford University Conservative Association on education.[13] Lighter activity came in the form of a cricket match against the Oxford University Liberal Club in June, in which Elaine took part. The OUDSC chair 'stressed the importance of winning' even in cricket.[14] Having proven herself an effective and competent participant in the club's college and university-level activities, at the start of Michaelmas term 1941, Elaine was elected as the OUDSC secretary.[15] The club chairman at that time was David Ginsburg, the future Labour (and Social Democratic Pary) MP for Dewsbury.

By now, Elaine was in her third and final year and the club was increasingly proactive in its support for women's rights (although it had had a women's officer since the beginning). In late November 1941, for example, the OUDSC executive agreed to pack the public gallery at the Oxford Union during a debate on the equality of the sexes in order to provide loud support for the movers of the motion.[16] But the circumstances of the war had changed significantly and the Soviet Union's entry, on the side of the allies, meant the reasons for the split between the OULC and the OUDSC had disappeared. Elaine joined the sub-committee of officers of both organisations which met to discuss their merger – the process took a significant amount of time, with several changes of committee members, and was not completed until 1943.[17] At the end of Michaelmas term 1941, Elaine was elected as chair of the OUDSC – the first woman to hold the post.[18] Her term began in January 1942.[19] Top of the list to invite to speak was Elaine's first choice: the veteran women's suffrage campaigner, Poplar councillor, and member of parliament, Susan Lawrence. Elaine recalled a 'tall white-haired woman, not only an executive member of the Labour Party but, as it turned out, a veteran of the "Votes for Women" campaign. [Lawrence] brought some stirring echoes of that earlier feminist solidarity to a generation that had virtually forgotten about it'.

With its official links to the Labour Party, the OUDSC provided undergraduates with insights into, and participation in, the development of Labour's ambition for life after the war. In January 1941, for instance, Clement Attlee spoke to the club of the need for 'plans for a new and fairer post-war world [which] could not be left to peace-time'. He continued:

> I do not think that after this war, we shall be able to afford an idle
> rich class. Equally, we shall not be able to afford to have those who
> are willing and able to work denied the opportunity. Unemploy-

ment must go.... We shall have swept away some evil things, such
as the family means test, widespread malnutrition and unemploy-
ment. We must see to it that they never come back.[20]

During Elaine's time at Oxford, the biggest name to appear – in
conjunction with the Oxford University English Club – was
George Orwell, who spoke at a combined meeting on 23 May
1941. His theme was 'Literature and Totalitarianism' – the same talk
had been given on the radio a few days before.[21] Elaine was (probably) a member of the English Club, too, attending its meetings on
Tuesday evenings – the OUDSC met on Fridays. This was a similarly well-connected environment and drew speakers from across
the literary world such as Dylan Thomas (who spoke in November
1941), John Betjeman, Stella Gibbons, and the editor of Penguin's
New Writing magazine John Lehmann. Whereas Kingsley Amis
was a significant figure in the Labour Club, serving as editor of its
Bulletin and as cultural secretary, the English Club was the main
stomping ground of Philip Larkin who enjoyed the attention given
to him by the mainly women undergraduates who filled the club's
ranks and its executive. Larkin served as treasurer. 'They used to
lionise Philip a bit', recalled one friend, 'asking him to tea and so
on. It was hard to say why, since he wasn't writing very much or
very well, but he was charismatic, you see. Girls wanted to find out
about him'.[22]

Not so Elaine, who seems never to have been particularly enthusiastic about either Amis or Larkin and instead found herself a very
different set of poetic friends: John Heath-Stubbs, Sidney Keyes,
Christopher Tosswill, and Drummond Allison. None of them, apart
from Tosswill, who was friendly with Amis, was particularly well dis-
posed to Larkin, either personally or in terms of poetry.[23] The dislike
between the rival poets was mutual, at least on the basis of letters

passed between Larkin and Amis at the time, and over time grew into something akin to hatred. Larkin was quite deliberately left out of the neo-Romantic *Eight Oxford Poets* collection edited by Keyes and Michael Meyer in 1941, and never let go of the snub. Heath-Stubbs recalled, that Larkin 'claimed forever after to be deeply offended by his exclusion, though it has to be said that the poems he submitted to Meyer were even earlier than his collection, *The North Ship*, which he subsequently disowned'.[24] Larkin could be his own worst enemy, of course. For a time he resisted the invitation of Fortune Press, and its owner R.A. Caton, to submit a volume of poetry for publication; the same invitation was taken up by Welsh poets Dylan Thomas and Nigel Heseltine, on the one hand, and by Drummond Allison, on the other. The latter's *The Yellow Night* appeared in 1944.

For Elaine these connections were more than coincidental, more than famous faces passed by in the street, and they were almost certainly the reason that Elaine enjoyed more of her time at Oxford than did Gwyn Thomas a decade earlier. These friendships, particularly with poets and aspirant politicians, provided intellectual and creative stimulation, potential opportunities (not least offers to stand as a parliamentary candidate for the Labour Party), and connections to a world very different from the South Wales Coalfield. The strongest relationship of all was with Drummond Allison. Elaine takes up the story,

> One day ... while walking along the pavement, I was accosted by Drummond Allison. I'd never met him before. He said he was planning to go for a walk with his friend Christopher Tosswill. It would be a long day out, they'd be taking sandwiches and he invited me to go with them. Well, why not?

Handsome and athletic, with a strong enthusiasm for cricket, acting and left-wing politics, as well as rhyme and metre, Allison was every bit the film star poet. He had already enjoyed a remarkably lively education at the private Bishop's Stortford College in Hertfordshire before arriving at Oxford in the same year as Elaine. As his biographer, Stephen Benson, records, Allison was involved in the school drama society, the branch of the League of Nations Union, the school choir, the debating society, served as editor of the school magazine, and was head of house. In the League of Nations Union branch meetings, members (including Allison) discussed pacifism and the Peace Pledge Union as well as a range of Left Book Club publications. Some of the schoolboys went on trips to the South Wales Coalfield to stay with the unemployed, and to learn about their experiences.[25]

Allison read history at the Queen's College and enjoyed a particularly close friendship with Heath-Stubbs, Tosswill and Keyes, all fellow Queensmen. They met regularly in Keyes's rooms, which overlooked Queen's College Lane and the St Edmund Hall graveyard, for gatherings they nicknamed 'the Salon'. These consisted of poetry readings and tea parties and were a place of creative expression for all those who attended, however reluctant they may have been to share their work. They were far more candid than the formality of the university English Club. Several of the products of 'the Salon' were published in the pages of the *Cherwell*, Oxford's literary magazine, and in book-length collections such as *Eight Oxford Poets*, and Ian Davie's 1943 selection *Oxford Poetry, 1942–1943*.[26] In his poetry, Allison cultivated an Audenesque aesthetic similar to Larkin, despite moving in generally anti-Auden circles, endowing some of his work with a clear political edge. In addition, he wrote essays for the *Cherwell* on figures such as T.H. White, film reviews, and plays which were performed by the Eglesfield Players of the Queen's College and by the Oxford University Labour

Club's drama group. Whether or not Elaine really did meet Allison for the first time walking down the street, or whether it was at the English Club, or even the OUDSC – Allison was appointed editor of the *Oxford Socialist* in March 1942[27] – the effect on her of that meeting was intoxicating. Elaine found herself immediately drawn to Allison and feel deeply in love.

According to her later recollection, Elaine first met Drummond Allison in her final year at Oxford, sometime between the autumn of 1941 and the spring of 1942. They certainly knew each other by Easter 1942, which that year fell in early April, given Elaine's detailed memory of the accident which caused a delay to Allison's military service, and allowed him to undertake one term's additional study of English literature.[28] The accident occurred at a performance given by the Eglesfield Players of Sidney Keyes's short play, 'The Prisoner'. Set in an imaginary Eastern European dictatorship in the aftermath of a fascist coup, Allison took the role of a captured communist. Just as he was dragged from the stage for his 'execution', the communist was pistol whipped by his captors – the action was much too realistic. Allison's head split open. Blood poured from the wound and he ended up in the Radcliffe Infirmary. Elaine recalled 'a small artery in his skull had been severed and his call-up was deferred. The delay irked him. He wasn't looking forward to the possibility of being killed – who would be? But he also had complicated worries about being seen not to be brave enough when it came to the crunch'.

The delay to Allison's callup occurred just as his closest friends were leaving to join the army: Sidney Keyes left at the end of Hilary Term, 1942. The absence was keenly felt. As Elaine put it later, 'exams were over. His friends were dispersing, mostly into the armed forces. He didn't want to go home, nor be alone in Oxford'. At first, perhaps, Elaine provided the company that Allison desired, not least because she was the more advanced student of English;

but friendship shared across novels and poems soon became something more amorous. Sadly, few details of their friendship have survived, fewer still of their romance: a handful of poems, a single letter now archived in Texas, and a painting by T.H. White, which Allison gifted to Elaine on his departure from Oxford for Sandhurst. White was a family friend and Allison had known him since childhood. Elaine, on the other hand, 'had just read and loved "The Sword in the Stone"', White's most famous novel first published in 1938. The painting showed a rotund general with curled moustache hanging precariously from an aircraft as it passed over fields and a scarlet castle. Around the general, gathering angels. A metaphor, perhaps, for the necessity of sundering a relationship in time of war.

Allison's poems to Elaine were written in the spring of 1942. The first, subsequently published in *The Yellow Night,* was titled *From Wales, Where Whistling Miners,* described the pair's return to Oxford from home – Pontypridd in Elaine's case, Surrey in Allison's case. Happy and content at being reunited, this was a poem for a close friend. The final poem in the sequence, *For Floyd,* was far more overt in its feeling.

> Through love, of thing or mind
> In Pontypridd or Purley.
>
> Be safe from any grave:
> Floyd be the favourite verb
> For lovers, and disturb
> Always the calm of hatred.

Years later, in her column for the *Western Mail,* Elaine reflected on her feelings for Drummond Allison and what had happened in the first months of 1942. This is what she wrote:

Was this 'the real thing'? The question has no relevance. There was a war on. There was plenty of amorous dalliance but neither of us used the word 'love' or saw the prospect of travelling the road of life together side by side and on into the sunset. That would certainly never have worked out. To borrow a phrase from the Beatles, I was somebody who at that difficult time made him feel all right. He made me feel all right too … Somebody else called him a life-enhancer. I'd go along with that.

Notice the insistence that 'neither of us used the word "love"' – this was a disguise on Elaine's part, as the poems from Drummond Allison illustrate. They *did* use the word love – and lovers – and the spirit conveyed is unmistakeable. Why else was Elaine the one person Allison wanted to be present as he passed out of Sandhurst? Throughout her long life, Elaine's first love was the one for whom she forever yearned. It was a longing made more poignant by Allison's departure from Oxford, his training at Sandhurst and then in Northern Ireland, and his active service in the Mediterranean theatre of war, but most especially by his death during the assault on Monte Camino in Italy on 2 December 1943. He was just twenty two.[29] Little more than six months earlier, Sidney Keyes had died on active service in Tunisia – it had a profound effect on Allison. Elaine's response to the news of Allison's death can only be guessed at but given all the evidence pointing to the depth of her affections, she undoubtedly felt the greatest pain. A pain which remained with her forever.

★ ★ ★

The news that Drummond Allison had been killed reached Elaine whilst she was living in Norfolk and working for the Workers' Educational Association in the county as a tutor-organiser. Her appointment had begun more than a year earlier, in September 1942, and had as much to do with the practicalities of maintaining adult education provision in wartime as with her own idealism – although that cannot be doubted. 'In peace time', she observed later, 'organisers would have applied to one of the men's colleges for recruits, but conscription had changed all that'. Together with two other graduates of Lady Margaret Hall, Elaine went out into the East Anglian countryside to deliver evening courses to 'men and women who'd had to leave school early and regretted it'.[30] The recruiters who arrived at Oxford in the summer of 1942 were Frank Jacques and John Hampden Jackson of the WEA's Eastern District.[31] Jacques was the District secretary and had been in that role since 1935, leading a transformation in the efficacy of adult education in a region where manual workers – the WEA's mainstay in the industrial north of England and South Wales – were much less significant a part of the population. As Vivian Williams noted in 1979, 'the District's activities had its widest appeal to non-manual occupations and housewives' although until the 1940s very few of the tutors themselves were women.

Jackson, the resident tutor in Norfolk, had been appointed by the Board of Extra Mural Studies at Cambridge University, and was a major influence in the development of the WEA in East Anglia. Jacques and Jackson appeared in Elaine's autobiographical writing as almost run of the mill organisers of education; in fact, the two men were amongst the most significant individuals in the WEA and British extra mural education in the middle of the twentieth century. A passionate and charismatic left-winger, Jackson's interests, and published scholarship ranged from British and European history to contemporary politics and international affairs.[32] He was later director of extra mural education at Cambridge. Jacques, on the other hand, had risen through the Railway Clerks Association and stood as a Labour Party candidate in 1924, 1929 and 1931, and thus focused his attention on WEA administration. He was to shape the careers of no lesser figures than Raymond Williams and E.P. Thompson, both of whom were first employed as adult educators by the Eastern District of the WEA.[33] As Jacques wrote of Williams, 'I should have hoped to use him, but he went away to Barnstaple to read and to write a novel, and we have lost one whose promise had filled us with great expectations'.[34] The novel, of course, was Williams's landmark *Border Country* poublished by Chatto & Windus in 1960.[35]

The focus of Elaine's teaching in Norfolk was contemporary affairs, perhaps following the suggestion of G.D.H. Cole that adult education classes should be considered as 'instruments for helping an important section of the public to think out its position in the light of current happenings'.[36] She delivered sessions on topics such as 'the formation of public opinion' (now a central function of media studies) and other matters relating to the hopes and aspirations of society in a postwar world. She turned some of the courses into lecture-length summaries delivered to organisations such as the Fabian Society, as well.[37] According to contemprary newspaper reports, Elaine put the case that public opinion was formed principally by the press, the radio, and the cinema – that is to say by the media and popular culture. It was an assessment framed by her already strong left-wing views. She insisted that 'the press and cinema too frequently put on capitalist propaganda and the press was not free, as popularly supposed'. This was hardly antithetical to the WEA at that time, nor to wider extra mural education, and similar themes were to find their way into Raymond Williams's studies of contemporary media in later decades, but Elaine never mentioned what she was teaching in her autobiographical writing. She carefully weeded out her more radical politics.

Life in Norfolk suited Elaine, she found herself revelling in work which shared many of the same characteristics as undergraduate study at Oxford – copious amounts of reading and the invocation of an argument to a discursive audience of the interested. It helped that teaching terms were short and ran only during the autumn and winter when agricultural work was slack. Just as at university, there was a long summer vacation when Elaine was free to seek alternative employment. 'One summer, for instance, I had felt an urge to experience London', she wrote, explaining that she duly took a job as a dishwasher in the underground shelter in Berkeley Square. At other times, Elaine came home to Pontypridd and looked after matters at 54 Telelkebir Road (including her elderly grandparents Fred and Martha) whilst Olive, her mother, went to work at the factories in Treforest. It was during one of those sojourns from Norfolk that, at a Beds for Stalingrad meeting, she encountered a young French teacher from Pontypridd Boys' Grammar School: Morien Waldo Parry Morgan.[38] In an interview with the *Western Mail* in 2013, Elaine explained that:

> I met my husband Morien at a political rally. He was very tall, dark and good at expressing himself. And also he was the first reasonable Communist I'd ever met... [A] year later we were married.

The encounter between Elaine and Morien was one of minds – of a shared commitment to the Left, to literature, to ideas – as much as of a soon-to-develop physical attraction. Morien was locally regarded as something of an expert on the Soviet Union and Joseph Stalin.[39] Four years older than Elaine he had avoided military service during the Second World War because of his poor eyesight. He had, however, served in Spain where he was captured by Francisco Franco's army and spent months in a prisoner of war camp at

San Pedro Cardeña in Burgos.[40] Born in Ynysybwl in 1916, Morien came from a highly political family, all of which was Labour supporting and had been instrumental in establishing branches of the Independent Labour Party and the Labour Party in the village. Morien's uncle, Abel Morgan, was a district councillor and a prominent figure in the Ynysybwl Co-operative Society; another uncle, Bethuel, a schoolmaster at Abercynon who died in 1925, had been a conscientious objector during the First World War; and his father, John E. Morgan was the secretary of the Lady Windsor Lodge of the South Wales Miners' Federation and one of the most well-known union officials in the coalfield.

Following in his father's footsteps, Morien had been heavily involved in Labour himself and served as chairman of the Ynyswbwl branch of the party in the 1930s. He was active, also, in the University of Wales Labour Federation.[41] As a student in Cardiff, however, Morien clandestinely joined the Communist Party becoming part of a circle of activists which included Will Paynter, Gilbert Taylor, Idris and Dora Cox, Len Jefferies, Alec Cummings, Sid Hamm, and Leo Abse – most of whom went to Spain in some capacity. Or had been to Moscow. In later years, Morien justified his choice by reference to the growing power of fascism in Germany – he had observed the militarisation of the Rhineland on a visit to Strasbourg in the mid-1930s and becamse convinced that appeasement was implausible and that the communist position of active confrontation was the correct approach. The outbreak of the Spanish Civil War radicalised him further and in his honours year he left to join the International Brigades.[42] After a difficult journey through France, including a period in a safe house in Carcassonne, he walked across the Pyrenees into Spain. After training at Guernica, Morien ended up in the machine gun company of the British Battalion and was involved in the retreat through Aragon in the winter of 1937-1938.

In an interview with the Imperial War Museum in 1987, Morien reflected on his experiences in Spain and the development of his political ideas, as well as their impact on his subsequent teaching career. At that time, he said, his views could be characterised as 'extreme left'. As a young teacher in Pontypridd in the Second World War, there was an attempt by some in the community to raise a petition to remove Morien from his post because of his politics, although he remained steadfastly non-political in the classroom: 'what else can you be', he explained to the interviewer, Conrad Wood, 'when you're teaching a language'. The threat of dismissal was neutralised, but it was not the last time Morien would face similar qualms about the likely imprint of his personal politics on his classroom activity. Each time his reply was the same – politics are left outside the chalkface. Perhaps that is what Elaine meant by her quip that Morien was the 'first reasonable communist' she had met. Outside the classroom, Morien found numerous ways of expressing his views and spoke frequently at meetings of organisations such as the Labour Party's League of Youth, the Anglo-Soviet Friendship Society, the Young Person's Guild, and (fortunately for Elaine) the Beds for Stalingrad campaign.

Support for the Soviet Union during the later stages of the Second World War, of course, was widespread and many ordinary people took an interest in the experiences of Britain's wartime ally. But there remained, still, a political inference which both Elaine and Morien understood – their mutual presence at campaign meetings were expressions of a worldview and of a leftist ideal. During the war, Elaine had moved to the left politically and was much less enthused by the moderate, social democratic politics of the men she had met at Oxford such as Roy Jenkins. She found in Morien someone who understood her ideas and the reasons behind them:

their coming together was serendipitous and the two quickly began courting. Like Drummond Allison, Morien was well-versed in literature and poetry – he had initially studied English, French and History at Cardiff, before switching to French – and his knowledge, as Elaine recalled later, 'seeped into the first letter he ever wrote to me'. All nineteen pages of it. Morien was very much Elaine's type. He was tall and dark, like Allison, with strong but handsome features; above all he was possessed of an intellectual curiosity and political certainty which Elaine prized. Given the circumstances of the war, it was a reasonably swift romance. Having met in the summer of 1943, the pair announced their engagement at Christmas 1944, and were married in Capel Rhondda, Hopkinstown, on 11 April 1945.[43]

★ ★ ★

Several months before, Morien had been appointed to a teaching post in Burnley, Lancashire.[44] He had already left Pontypridd early in 1944, taking a job at Hamond's Grammar School in Swaffham in Norfolk, in order to be closer to Elaine. She was still teaching with the WEA. The pair spent most weekends together – Swaffham being some thirty miles away from Diss, where Elaine was living. Marriage marked the end of Elaine's association with the Eastern District of the WEA and she resolved to join Morien in Lancashire as soon as she could. Burnley, rather than Pontypridd or Norfolk, was Morien's choice – he had insisted on setting up an independent household in a new environment, perhaps to prove to his parents that he was able to survive without their support or their influence. Burnley, being so far away from South Wales, offered that freedom. Elaine and Morien lived initially in lodgings before eventually being granted an unfurnished part of a house: 44 Prestwich Street, which they shared with two old ladies. Married life started out with a 'bed, table, four chairs, and a couple of tea chests supplied gratis by the nearest grocer'.[45] Although, by the time Dylan, their eldest son, was born in May 1946, Elaine and Morien had taken possession of the entire house. The older women had been found alternative accommodation.[46]

Life in Lancashire was less of a disturbance to Elaine and Morien's routine than has traditionally been supposed. In her autobiographical writings, and in interviews, Elaine gave the impression that moving north marked the end of her teaching career and the start of her life as a mother and as a houswife. This is not what happened. In fact, despite having young children, Elaine's life in Burnley was far more frenetic than it had been in Norfolk. Careful examination of the newspapers for the town reveals that from the autumn of 1945 until the family left Burnley to return to South Wales five years later, Elaine was active as a public speaker and teacher with the Women's Co-operative Guild, the WEA, the United Nations Association, the Communist Party, and the Extra Mural Department of Manchester University. In other words, she steadfastly maintained her career as an adult educator, often working alongside Morien in the same community networks. This was also the period in which her feminism began to assert itself, not least in her work to establish international women's day celebrations in the north west of England and in her teaching about women's industrial employment.

But why disguise or alter her life story? What purpose did it serve? The relative absence of the truth in Elaine's portrait of her life in Lancashire was part of a well-constructed identity designed initially for audiences in the 1950s and 1960s little used to the kind of social mobility which Elaine had experienced. In later years, having developed a life of its own, it suited Elaine to be thought of as a housewife with innate talents and as the provincial outsider who was able to break into metropolitan literary and creative circles. Both impressions fulfilled romantic notions, summed up in the persona of the housewife-dramatist adopted by Elaine in the 1950s, and amplified the idea that it was luck rather than dogged determination and ability which had sustained a long career as a writer and broadcaster. Leaving out her political fervour and the significance of adult education in crafting her worldview and her approach to delivering her message meant that Elaine sacrificed some of the status afforded to her male colleagues. Yet, for her, no less than Gwyn Thomas in the 1930s and Raymond Williams from 1946 until the start of the 1960s, experience as an adult educator was formative.

Adult education in the industrial north was quite different from Elaine's previous experience in East Anglia, and in the view of some in contemporary WEA circles it was regarded as closer to the spirit of the movement. Tutors were teaching the industrial proletariat, as it were, rather than (as some believed) would-be country squires.[47] Almost immediately that Elaine moved to Burnley, to be with Morien, she began teaching for the local branches of the WEA and the National Council of Labour Colleges (NCLC). Her first post was as tutor for the Hapton branch of the WEA a few miles outside of Burnley. Morien, at that time, was tutor for the Burnley branch of the NCLC.[48] It was very much a joint effort between a husband and wife who shared a left-wing critique of capitalism and took a critical stance towards the post-war Labour government. Elaine and Morien's activities were readily reported in the divisional roundups in the NCLC's *Plebs* magazine and in the WEA's *The Highway*.[49] Topics taught included postwar reconstruction, local government, and economics, and were apt to the debate around the rebuilding of Britain and the nature of Clement Attlee's 'New Jerusalem'.

Morien recalled later that 'Elaine and I lectured on social studies and international affairs ... and we always used to pride ourselves on presenting a very objective viewpoint of things'. [50] Given his other contract at Burnley Grammar School where he was employed to teach French and social affairs, Morien's extra mural teaching was the more straightforward of the two. He was a tutor for the NCLC and taught evening classes at Burnley Municipal College – a pattern of adult education he would repeat, later, when living and teaching in Aberillery.[51] Elaine's career was more varied but was, in broad terms, a continuation of her work in East Anglia. Following her year as tutor-organiser for the WEA's Hapton branch, she moved on to join the Padiham branch where her theme was local government and topics included the development of Britain's public health system.[52] This was Elaine's contribution to the debate which accompanied the introduction of the National Health Service. By 1947, she had become a tutor with the WEA's branch in Nelson but also worked for Manchester University's extra mural department in the town delivering classes in current affairs and international relations. She held that role for two years, leaving in 1949. [53]

Extra mural teaching encouraged and enabled a high level of participation in public affairs and Elaine became a regular – and at times controversial – correspondent to the local press, notably the *Burnley Express*. One such press controversy concerned a lecture she delivered to the NCLC in the autumn of 1946 in which she called for the nationalisation of the BBC. There were, she argued, 'certain dangers in BBC administration without Parliamentary control, whereby the British public might not know what was happening in such important branches as broadcasts to foreign countries'. This was then followed by a discussion of the 'political development' of the corporation and for a plea to reconsider the idea of 'wired wireless' installed in every home.[54] Writing in response, 'Radiorelay', an enthusiast of the *Daily Mail*, dismissed nationalisation of the BBC as 'that remedy for all the ills of the flesh beloved of the bureaucratic-minded and those who love to direct the lives of others "for their own good" of course'.[55] Elaine's response was to lay out more clearly her political reasoning for socialising the economy, rather than simply nationalising from above:

> I appear to have touched 'Radiorelay' on the raw with my remarks to the NCLC. Certainly "private enterprise" relay is cheaper than Capt. Eckersley's scheme would have been at the outset. One reason is that his plan would have provided a choice of all programmes sent out by the BBC – ultimately seven or eight, each broadcasting all day in a special field, drama, sport, religion, variety or news and news talks on the lines of the new "third programme"; while Burnley people are still being asked to be patient about their second choice. The war is blamed for this, but if Burnley was a "pioneer" relay town it must have lost its pioneering spirit very quickly.
>
> Other districts had their second programme years before the war. The other reason for the cheapness of local relay is that when the BBC decided not to take over the relays it reserved the right to change its mind after two years. So that private relay firms, fearing early confiscation, stuck to a policy of quick returns, and were unwilling to sink more capital into improving their networks. I do not know whether this is why Burnley relays faltered in their forward march. But we do know that now, wherever the second programme is introduced, the cost to the consumer is doubled. At this rate, how cheaply could private enterprise have provided eight alternatives?
>
> Clearly, if the BBC had consented to administer a relay at the same level of efficiency as the one we enjoy, they could have done it more cheaply, if only by saving the expense of door-to-door col-

lectors and putting the cost in with the licence money. And they might not have found it necessary to charge a new tenant for re-wiring the relay system when the tenant moving out was already enjoying the service. In any case, the reference to "vested interests" was not an attack on private relays. The chief opposition to Eckersley must have come not from the newly-founded relays but from the wireless firms who would have faced bankruptcy. How many people would buy wireless sets if they could get all the foreign stations from a loud-speaker only?

As to the taking over of the original British Broadcasting Company, I share your correspondent's sympathy for the firms concerned. Before that time they were indeed sitting pretty. With a guaranteed monopoly to shield them from the competition that enlivens American radio, with the GPO to collect their licence money for them, and yet with complete independence, they enjoyed just the degree of "state interference" that every capitalist dreams of.

Finally, may I explain that I used the BBC as an example of how not to nationalise. At present it enjoys Government protection without responsibility to Parliament. No MP can ask questions about it. They need only "satisfy the Postmaster-General". Perhaps his assistant, Mr Burke [Burnley's MP], will tell us one day what that entails. If the Labour Government follows the pattern of the BBC, the London Public Transport Board and the Central Electricity Board in any new industries it takes over it might "nationalise" our whole economy without Socialising anything. [56]

The debate between Elaine and Radiorelay continued across several editions, focusing on the division between private enterprise, nationalisation and socialisation. At its heart was the rejection, by Radiorelay, of the Fabian system of state planning in favour of a co-operative model. As Radiorelay explained,

> I sang on the platforms of H.M. Hyndman in the Clarion Choir long ago, before many of the present-day so-called Socialist

careerists were born. I am not a Tory, but I still know common-
sense when I read it. My home table was good enough, too, for
George Lansbury and Jack Jones and I can tell a few stories of the
back of the scenes of the early "brothers" of the Socialist movement which would curl the hair of those who heard them.[57]

He continued a few weeks later, laying out his contempt for the
current Labour government and its instincts:'These Fabian planners
have proved their utter incompetence to plan for an era of plenty.
They can only plan a state of shortages for all'.[58] Elaine did not
reply. Nevertheless, the debate illustrates some of her political views
in this formative period.

Nationalisation was not the only consideration. With the return
to peacetime conditions, women found themselves pushed out of
work and, where they remained, subject to wildly differing rates of
pay compared with their male counterparts. It was a topic which
Elaine took up with vigour, foreshadowing her participation in the
women's liberation movements of the 1970s. Speaking to the
Burnley Co-operative Men's Guild in the spring of 1947, she set
out her case:

> If the services of married women in remunerative employment
> were to be secured, they should be allowed to do part-time work
> on terms of equal pay with men. Working conditions in Lancashire,
> however, were different from those in other parts of the country,
> and Lancashire must be excepted from any generalisation. The Lan-
> cashire attitude towards women going out to work was somewhat
> different from that in other parts of the British Isles and in Lan-
> cashire, in peacetime, normally forty three per cent of women went
> out to work.
>
> The two world wars had, of course, brought great changes but
> the percentage of the female working population had hardly
> changed during the last eighty years. Eighty years ago, twenty five

per cent of women were in employment. Today the figure was twenty seven per cent. Although just as few women were working for wages, however, they were working in a wider variety of jobs. The trend had been away from domestic service and towards industry and commerce. With certain limitations, such as the medical profession, women had today taken their place in nearly every field.

The main thing for which women were now fighting was equal pay. Many false arguments were adduced to combat the claim. It was suggested, for instance, that women were "less efficient" than men; but it would not be overlook that male workers were not themselves equally efficient, yet two men, one efficient and one inefficient – or not so efficient – were given equal pay.

Women tended to crowd into the lower-paid jobs and therefore, because of the competition, an employer could successfully offer a lower wage. Male workers, too, were willing and able to travel up and down the country looking for the jobs they wanted, but parents were unwilling to allow their parents to do so; also, women workers were not so well organised as men. For a variety of good reasons, women did not have such good trade unions as male workers.

She concluded the talk, however, by lamenting that whereas equal pay for women was bound to come in time, the Labour Party had been 'very backward' on this issue.[59] As an organiser of women, as well as a speaker, Elaine was most active in the Burnley organising committee for International Women's Day, which she helped to establish late in 1945, in the Co-operative men's and women's guilds, and as inaugural chair of the Burnley branch of the United Nations Association on its creation in 1947.[60] The UNA's first major public debate, over which Elaine presided, considered the formation of a unified Europe and was held at the town's central library in September 1947.[61]

By all accounts, Elaine's life in Burnley was extremely busy and as occupied with teaching and political activism as it was with domestic duties and motherhood. She might have settled there permanently but for the decision taken by Morien in about 1949 to seek a return to South Wales, ostensibly because of Dylan's ill health. Elaine wrote, later, 'Dylan developed symptoms of asthma, and the doctor said that Burnley's climate and situation, while ideal for the cotton industry, was bad for respiratory disease'. Dylan's asthma began the conversation about moving away, the onset of asthma in Gareth, their newborn second son, convinced Elaine and Morien of the necessity of leaving Lancashire. Morien recalled the situation in the interview with the Imperial War Museum, noting that as part of his teaching and public speaking duties he had been studying the health impact of pollution on the resident population for some time prior to the family's departure. Burnley, he learned from close study of medical officer's reports, was the fourth most polluted town in the industrial north-west of England, with Manchester at the top of the list.[62] It was evidence enough they had to find somewhere to live. Just as it had been Morien's decision to move north, so it was his decision to leave, Elaine simply had to follow.[63]

Morien found work at Abertillery Grammar School teaching languages, which enabled the family to move south. It was neither an easy transition, nor a straightforward one. The family had nowhere suitable to live either in or near Abertillery before term started and so Morien settled into lodgings whilst Elaine moved back to Hopkinstown with Dylan and Gareth. She found temporary work teaching English at her former secondary school, which at least provided her with a separate income for a time. Eventually, Morien managed to find somewhere for the family to live: an isolated farmhouse on a hillside in the Marches. With a scant population, little by way of public transport, and no demand for university extension classes or the WEA, none of the activities to which Elaine had devoted so much of her life since leaving Oxford were possible. It was a lonely period. As she explained later, 'I didn't have a lot of people, I couldn't go and talk to my sisters because I was an only child'.[64] With her career as a lecturer over, for the time being, at least, Elaine turned to her other great passion: writing. Inspired by the countryside around her and with ample time and few distractions, particularly with her children at school, Elaine found living in the Marches conducive to creativity. It was to be as a writer that she made her name.

THREE
SIGNED, E.M.

An isolated farmhouse high on the mountainside, just inside the Welsh border, was an unlikely venue from which to launch a career as a writer and broadcaster, but this was how Elaine claimed to have started out in the early 1950s. As she put it many years later, 'we lived in rural Radnorshire ... miles away from any other house. Morien would go away on Monday and come back on Saturday and I was up there feeding the chickens and milking the goat ... I started writing little stories about that kind of life and background and I started selling them'. Morien was teaching nearly thirty miles away in Abertillery and travelled back and forth to the countryside each weekend on his motorbike. The farmhouse was called 'The Birches' and lay a few miles from the small Herefordshire village of Michaelchurch Escley, itself some fifteen miles west of Hereford and ten miles south of Hay on Wye. Except, of course, that was not how it all began – the farmhouse and the hillside loneliness were part and parcel of the carefully constructed mythos of Elaine Morgan, the housewife dramatist whose career was as accidental as it was successful. But if not this way, how did Elaine really start out?

In the spring of 1950, whilst still living in Pontypridd, Elaine sent a script entitled 'Words for Women' to the BBC marked for the attention of Gale Pedrick – the creator, in 1959, of the radio highlights programme *Pick of the Week.* Pedrick's secretary replied on 9 May, explaining that they would pass along the script to the producers of *Woman's Hour*.[1] It did not, however, end up at *Woman's Hour* but was instead passed to the script section of the Variety Department. It was they who explained to Elaine that although they found the 'sketch on the whole very amusing' and in the style of *Take It From Here*, Denis Norden and Frank Muir's pioneering comedy series, it would be hard for her to find much work as a freelance writer with Variety because it was

> difficult to make use of writers who live so far away from the centre of broadcasting as you do yourself. This is in no sense through any desire on the part of the BBC to employ only London writers, but is brought about by the nature of the Variety Department's task, entailing as it does constant conference between artists, producer and writers.[2]

The script was passed on once again, this time to Mai Jones, producer of *Welsh Rarebit* at BBC Wales, with the encouragement that 'the writer has a definite turn for comedy'.[3] Elaine was soon invited to visit the studios in Cardiff. The result, after all the to-ing and fro-ing, an offer to broadcast a segment on *Woman's Hour* in the autumn of 1950. It was called 'Let's Do An Experiment' and was transmitted on 26 October, little more than a week before her thirtieth birthday.[4] Elaine travelled to Cardiff once more to begin rehearsals at midday, with a view to live broadcast from two o'clock. At the time, *Woman's Hour* was presented by Jean Metcalfe, who had begun her career at the BBC as a typist before moving to Forces Radio where she gained a reputation as the 'speaking Vera Lynn'. Elaine's first words on that Thursday afternoon, the first she ever spoke on the radio, were these:

Although my father was unemployed for many years when I was a child, they were among the happiest of my life. While he was working in the pit, he had built himself a shed in the backyard as a workshop, and now that he had nothing else to do, he became general handyman to the neighbourhood. He would mend clocks and watches, windows and drains; people brought their children's boots to be mended, hair to be cut, splinters to be extracted; lame hedgehogs or grass snakes rescued from their tormentors, all arrived at our house for healing.[5]

She went on to describe a series of science experiments which her father, Billy Floyd, had taught her in that shed. It was a loving portrait of a man who had been dead more than ten years, and a nod to Elaine's life-long passion for science. By the time of the broadcast, Elaine had already moved to Herefordshire and was living in a house in the small village of Peterchurch, twelve miles outside Hereford. For her efforts, she earned eight pounds and eight shillings, or around three hundred pounds today.[6] Elaine's second broadcast on *Woman's Hour,* this time from the Birmingham studio, came in April 1951. The script described the experience of taking her children out to tea at a restaurant and was called 'My Embarrassing Half-Hour'. She followed it up with further embarrassing tales in 'The Thing', which featured on *Woman's Hour* in December 1951.[7] Then in March 1952, Elaine provided a script detailing her experience of living in that remote farmhouse, 'Roses Round the Door'.[8] She told listeners that:

> At the end of last October we moved into the Birches. I hadn't seen the house myself, but it sounded lovely; an old farmhouse, on a hilltop, solid stone, with lots of oak beams and big bedrooms with sloping ceilings. There was a dairy, too, a paddock with seven pine trees, and strawberries running wild in the garden. And just outside the door, a trellis of roses. Of course, they wouldn't be out at the

end of October, but still – roses. It would be heaven ... I felt like
one of the pioneer women of covered wagon days.

By the mid-1950s, Elaine had provided *Woman's Hour* with more
than half a dozen scripts and was reasonably well-known as an
effective contributor to programmes directed at women. But the
studio call was intermittent – three scripts in 1951 and one each in
1952, 1953, and 1954. With broadcasting so infrequent, Elaine
turned to other avenues to make money, not least the writing competitions at the back of the *New Statesman* and *The Observer's*
essay prize, which she won in December 1952.[9] In her memoir,
she explained that writing poems and brief fictional sketches – the
competitive demands of the *New Statesman* – helped to pass some
of the time spent alone at the farmhouse. 'Morien would bring
home reading matter including a weekly copy of the *New Statesman* and the previous Sunday's *Observer*', she recalled, 'I began
sending in entries to the competition at the back'. Amongst the
earliest of these was published at the beginning of January 1951
and was a response to a problem set by the novelist V.S. Pritchett
(writing under his pseudonym, Richard Lister): to compose 'an
extract ... from the report by a Polynesian anthropologist on the
Christmas customs of the English'. Elaine wrote:

> At the winter solstice they embark on a period of feasting once
> intended to see them through months of torpor. The recrystallising
> into almost disintegrated family units suggests that whole families
> hibernated together (cf. certain snakes) in holes dug in the ground
> and roofed with branches. They still festoon their ceilings with the
> few green products of now deciduous woodlands.
>
> When the individual had gorged to capacity, he would give
> away any remaining food which would not keep until spring, his
> descendants still use this season for giving away unwanted trifles.

They believe that Santa Claus, (Lat. *clausus*, shut up or enclosed)
god of hibernation, enters their houses via the chimney, recalling
when the only entry to the winter home was from above. Following the main feast day comes "Boxing Day," the day for retiring to
the "box" or lair (cf. the obsolete "give you good den.")

The traditional Christmas pantomimes show the hibernation
theme clearly (Sleeping Beauty, Babes in the Wood), more recent
ones obliquely (Aladdin's Cave, Peter Pan's underground house,
Alice down the rabbit hole).

The hardier northern tribes had a shorter period of hibernation
and began feasting as much as a week later.

She signed her entry, E.M.[10]

This was one of dozens of successful entries, published both in
the *New Statesman* and more infrequently in *The Spectator* until
the mid-1950s, which won Elaine prizes of a few guineas at a time.
She eventually dropped the quasi-pseudonymous 'E.M.' and signed
her work using her own name and began appearing elsewhere in
the magazine as a correspondent, essayist, and eventually as a
contributor-reviewer. The large body of work which Elaine created,
and which was published in the pages of the *New Statesman*, especially, has long been forgotten, but at the time it caught the eye of
BBC producers and gave renewed impetus to her broadcasting
career – particularly for radio. The man responsible for that revival
was Aled Vaughan, then the Welsh Region's general content producer. He wrote to Elaine, on the advice of the Head of Welsh
Programmes, Alan Watkin Jones, in mid-June 1954 inviting her to
'indulge in ...'"sporadic free-lance writing'" and promising to accept
the script he hoped would follow.[11] She wrote back offering a
number of options: something on the atomic bomb, which prefig-
ured Elaine's later Ban the Bomb activism, a talk on Welsh medium
education, or a script more akin to the autobiographical segments

previously broadcast on *Woman's Hour*. Vaughan settled for the first of these, which appeared on the Welsh Home Service on 10 August 1954 as *Reprieve?* It was produced by Selwyn Roderick.[12]

Independent of Aled Vaughan's invitation and her own response, Elaine had sent into the Cardiff studios a script called 'beginner's Welsh' all about her experiences learning the language. Nan Davies, the producer at the Bangor studio who first read it, thought Elaine's offering 'rather strange'. Nevertheless, it was passed to the Head of Welsh Programmes with the encouragement that 'this talk might make a most interesting broadcast'.[13] Watkin Jones had little enthusiasm for the idea:

> Mrs Morgan would be preaching as it were to the converted who would derive no pleasure surely in listening to someone maltreating spoken Welsh, however much sympathy we sometimes feel like bestowing upon beginners. And, after all, why should we get excited because an English woman, married to a Welshman living in Wales, should decide to learn our language?[14]

A few days before *Reprieve?* was broadcast, ironically given the internal discussion at the BBC, Elaine appeared in the *Western Mail* for calling for the extension of Welsh medium education to secondary schools. Speaking at a meeting of the National Union of Parents Association, she called on parents to make the most of Welsh medium schools and declared that 'it was in a Welsh school her own children would have the most valuable education'.[15] Dylan and Gareth had both been educated at Ysgol Gynradd Gymraeg Aberdâr. In her view, the Welsh education system 'as far as the teaching of Welsh was concerned was quite solid up to the 11-plus stage. After that it became threadbare and was solid again when a boy or girl went to college'. She had previously written an article for *The Highway*, the national magazine of the Workers' Educational Association, on the same question. 'There is a spirit in these schools', she wrote of the Welsh medium primaries, 'which I have not encountered in anything else under the aegis of the LEAs'. She continued:

> You feel it in the meetings of the parents' associations – which are apt to meet in the top room over an Italian ice-cream shop and discuss their problems keenly over coffee and biscuits – and which have already federated into a National Association. You feel it in the inter-valley concerts performed by the children, where parents and supporters fill a large hall and a double tier of galleries, and applaud news of the schools' progress, not with a polite spatter of Speech Day claps, but with irrepressible fervour. And you feel it in the schools, where the education is of that warm, rather exciting kind only offered by people who are moved by a 'passionate idea'.[16]

Elaine's belief in the value and validity of Welsh-medium education never wavered – she was a prominent figure in the parents association in Aberdare – and the politics of the campaign to extend provision pushed her sympathies close in tone to those of contemporary Welsh nationalism but never into the ranks of Plaid Cymru.

By 1955, Elaine had established a developing career as a lecturer, broadcaster, and writer. The latter aspect, aside from script work for the BBC, has been under-appreciated largely because so much of Elaine's creative output – in the form of short stories and poems – has been neglected. In truth, she wrote and secured publication of several short stories in the 1950s in magazines primarily targeted at women including *My Weekly* and *Homes and Gardens*. Much like her *Woman's Hour* scripts, they were autobiographical in foundation, taking what had been real-life situations and fictionalising them. 'Five Day Week', published in *My Weekly* in September 1953, was a typical story. It told of Geraldine Carey, a frustrated young mother whose isolated life in a countryside farmhouse far from any suburb, and her experiences trying to maintain a friendly disposition towards her toddler son 'Scrap'. 'For five days a week Scrap was Mummy's boy, good as gold. But at the weekend he was Daddy's boy, as unpredictable as an atom bomb', explained the blurb.[17] The story was a variant on the Rose Cottage segment broadcast on *Woman's Hour* a few months earlier and featured a similar panic about a toddler lost on the hillside.

Although they were competent short stories, befitting the context of their publication and their target audience, they were by no means classics of the genre. Today, they are primarily of interest because of what they reveal about Elaine's own life and her thoughts on motherhood, as well as forming a small collection of creative writing not intended for broadcast. More compelling, in many ways, are the poems written for the *New Statesman* which hint at Elaine's domestic discontent. In February 1954, around the nadir of her marriage to Morien, she penned the following, rather blunt, angry and thinly disguised poem:

> By the U-bend that is blocked, by the cock that's
> >   uncocked,
> By my leak-plugging finger, don't loiter! don't
> >   linger!
> By the terror that is stealing across my poor ceiling
> By the bellying plaster, come faster! come faster !'[18]

A short time previously, by now living back in Wales – at Abernant, near Aberdare – Elaine had discussed with Morien the possibility of having a third child; she harboured a desire for a daughter. Morien, however, had little desire for more children and had been quite reluctant even to have a second, let alone a third. The first signal that all was not well in the marriage came with this pastiche of the famous Rudyard Kipling poem, *If.* It was published in the

New Statesman in June 1951 and titled simply, 'For a Girl'.

> If you can queue and not be tired by queueing,
> Never be rushed, yet let no meal be late;
> If you can sit and hear what he's been doing,
> And not jump up to put the mirror straight;
> If you can fry an egg while all about you
> Shout for lost studs, books, marbles, and the
> pot; If you aren't hurt when they can do without you,
> Nor cross when, once you're busy, they cannot;
>
> If you can feel, while washing baby's nappy,
> Blest that the tender task's vouchsafed to you;
> If you can smile to see your son so happy
> Exploring with a broom the parlour flue;
> If you wear clothes that are both cheap and lasting,
> Nor once regret the might-have-been career,
> Then, for a good man's love, thank heaven fasting.
> If not, you'd better drop the whole idea.[19]

The poem marked the first time Elaine signed her full name at the base of her contributions. In her memoir, she explained that this was due to confusion amongst long-term readers as to who 'E.M.' could be – not least the powerful and influential civil servant, Sir Edward Marsh, who had previously used the moniker. This may well have been true, and it may also have reflected her desire for 'presence' following successful *Woman's Hour* appearances, but it was also the case that Elaine emerged from the pseudonymous shadows just as her anger about Morien's intransigence in relation to more children was rising. On the one hand, why hide any longer when there was a career to be had? On the other, what better way to make pointed comments about her marriage? After all, without the disguise Morien could be in little doubt as to the message Elaine was trying to convey. Imagine his reaction to reading:

> *To Macbeth* – Your wife, having experienced motherhood and knowing how tender it is, nevertheless has avoided another pregnancy because you once insisted she bring forth men-children only, and this she cannot ensure. Never forget that women have literal minds...[20]

Elaine's fury had been prompted by the 'deal' made with Morien to secure his agreement to try for a third child. He would accede only if Elaine was able to earn one thousand pounds as a 'deposit' and set the sum aside to support the extension of the family. Morien gambled on it being enough of a barrier, financially, or that it would take long enough to raise the money that the couple's advance into middle age would make it less likely that Elaine would be able to conceive. This was by no means folly: the sum would be the equivalent of more than twenty five thousand pounds today – in the region of double the average annual salary at the time and about fifty per cent more than the price of the average car. Elaine, of course, saw it as a surmountable challenge. One of her last poems for the *New Statesman*, published at the end of October 1954, pointed a way forward:

> Next winter, say, we'll take a buggy an' ride,
> A cute one – pink, with drapes an' things in blue;
> Just you an' me, honey, all snug inside,
> With kissin' corners you can sink into.
>
> You'll shut your eyes, 'cause you'd be leery, I reckon,
> Of lookin' out the winders, case you seen
> A ruck of hants an' such peek in an' beckon,
> Devils and wolves maybe – all black, an' mean.

Then you'll feel sump'n tickle you – like this –
An' run acrost your neck. You'll think: a kiss?
Naw, some fool bug or spider, I'll be bound.

"Ketch it!" you'll say, an' bend your head down low
We'll take our time a-hunting for it though.
Say, babe, that crittur cert'nly gits around...[21]

Elaine's true feelings about the situation might have been lost forever but for the survival of a remarkable set of letters penned under the pseudonym, 'Angharad', an oblique reference to Pontypridd, and submitted to the Co-operative Correspondence Club. Formed in 1936 by a group of women in response to a letter published in the mothering magazine *Nursery World* the previous year, the Co-operative Correspondence Club was, ostensibly, a women's mutual aid organisation. The letter, which stimulated the club's formation, was a plea for help not much different from Elaine's own experiences in the farmhouse: 'I live a very lonely life as I have no near neighbours. I cannot afford to buy a wireless ... I get so down and depressed after the children are in bed and I am alone in the house'. After being inundated with responses, the original letter writer (who used the nom de plume, Ubique) established the organisation. Elaine was one of the last to join, entering the circle of correspondents in the early 1950s – she was invited when one of the older members read her writings in the *New Statesman* and thought that they chimed with the club's aims and objectives.

Elaine made the most of the quasi-anonymity of the club and poured out her feelings on sexuality and motherhood, feelings which she kept away from Morien – who, in any case, she felt, did not really understand. The private discussion was different in tone to the public presentation of the same issues, of course, but both came from the same source of pain. In September 1955, having built up the confidence to discuss the subject, Elaine told the other members about the 'deposit' which Morien had insisted upon:

> From ancestry to the hope of progeny. When I mentioned this in one issue, two of you scribbled helpful hints to me, viz. 'Ever thought of tempting him?' and 'Or cheating him?' Neither of these is any good to me. You see, in our menage, the control of this side of things has never been left to the distaff side. Believe it or not, to the best of belief and knowledge I have never even *beheld* a 'wife's best friend' or whatever you call it, still less learned how to manipulate one. I think this was first because he thought I would be inefficient and later because he found I was recklessly philo-progenitive and quite capable of filling his house with noisy pledges of my affection while blandly protesting every time that I didn't know the gun was loaded...
>
> However, now he has ten years' expertise in keeping us both very happy and contented with no risk. (Please don't anyone scribble questions on *this* one, as I am already blushing hotly.) Once he used to rely partly on dates, and then I could cheat a bit, and did, hence Gareth – so now he doesn't. I can tempt him easily enough, but he just joyfully succumbs, and a good (but alas! Unproductive) time is had by all.
>
> No, I must just earn that thousand, then he won't go back on his word. I'll keep you in touch with the score. Actually, I have just made the first century – like this. £25 I have saved from the TV play in the spring, £25 came very belatedly (luckily- otherwise it would have gone on holidays) from the WEA for a course last winter, and I have just had a contract for £56 for *The Tamer Tamed*, the play Welsh Regional is broadcasting next month. £6 to give away, £50 to put away= £100.[22]

The television play referred to was her debut, *Mirror, Mirror,* which aired on 20 March 1955, and starred Brenda Hogan, Sylvia Marriott, and the popular character actor Bernard Lee.[23] Unfortunately, the programme met with a poor reception from the critics and (as she was to later suggest) almost ended her scriptwriting career before it had really begun. Elaine was writing for a medium about which she knew relatively little given the family did not yet own a television, an experience which she used as the basis of her teleplay *Without Vision* broadcast in July 1956.[24] Writing in the *Liverpool Echo*, one reviewer pondered of *Mirror, Mirror* 'can hypnotism be a subject for fun?' He concluded, that the play 'foundered somewhere between Svengali, Snow White, Freud and farce'.[25] The review for the industry journal, *The Stage*, was less forgiving and declared *Mirror, Mirror* 'a wearisome little affair', although this undoubtedly reflected a certain disbelief in the feminist central message of the play: that beauty is an affliction and masculine attention potentially dangerous.[26]

★ ★ ★

More than a year before the broadcast of *Mirror, Mirror*, Elaine had written to broadcasting house offering quite a different screenplay – 'The Golden World' – all about the domestication of Robin Hood and Maid Marian. It was not, however, well received by those who read it at the BBC – they thought it an 'incredibly boring play mainly consisting of long scenes of wrangling between Robin Hood, Marian and Friar Tuck'. Elaine, it was said, 'may have the art of essay writing but I see no promise as a dramatist'.[27] Fortunately, programme makers in Cardiff were far more forgiving and saw far more promise: the twin disasters of the unmade Robin Hood story and *Mirror, Mirror* did not derail *The Tamer Tamed*, which was picked up by the Welsh Home Service in the autumn of 1955 and transposed to television in Britain and the Netherlands a few months later.[28] Behind the scenes, perhaps ignoring attitudes towards Elaine's other writings, executives at the Home Service thought the script offered a 'clever frolic'.[29] Others were much less convinced, finding the plot 'thin and rather pointless'.[30] The range of responses from enthusiastic to hostile indicate that although Elaine's career as a scriptwriter did eventually take off, at times, particularly in the mid-1950s, it was a close-run-thing.

A week before *The Tamer Tamed* went out on the radio, Elaine received the news that her play *Wilde West* had won a competition for would-be television dramatists held as part of the 1955 Cheltenham Literature Festival.[31] With a guarantee that the script would be filmed, Elaine had earned herself a second chance on television – a way of wiping away the bad memories left by the failure of *Mirror, Mirror*. *Wilde West* focused on Oscar Wilde's 1889 tour of the United States and imagined Wilde, played by Peter Sallis, stuck in a log cabin after becoming stranded when the wheel of his carriage goes awry. Unable to complete his journey until morning, Wilde found himself entertaining the local hillbillies. Not everyone found this teleplay successful either. Peter Black, writing in the *Daily Mail*, thought the writing had been over-stretched and felt that Sallis 'in a Harry Secombe wig' had been miscast.[32] The sentiments were echoed by the *Daily Telegraph* which concluded that 'the play was flat and overlong'.[33] Welsh reviewers, however, were far more encouraging. Elaine's prize and her breakthrough onto television gave the *Western Mail* the opportunity – then very rare – to declare that 'in Elaine Morgan Wales has provided TV with a playwright who has a sharp eye for characterisation and a keen ear for dramatic dialogue'.[34]

Still, though, there were the wildly divergent perceptions of Elaine's abilities to deal with, perceptions which had the potential to jeopardise her fledgeling career. Importantly, one of those most supportive of Elaine's talent was the head of the script department

at television centre, Donald Wilson, and if there was any single producer at the BBC who might be credited with guiding Elaine's
fortunes in this period and steering her towards success – it was
him. In the 1960s, Wilson would go on to co-create *Doctor Who*
and adapt John Galsworthy's epic *The Forsyte Saga* for television,
but in 1955 he was fresh in post and keen to make an impact
through new writing. Elaine fitted the bill. In a memo to Michael
Barry, then head of television drama, Wilson explained that he
thought Elaine an

> interesting vital character [albeit] with, at present, too much leaning
> towards period stuff. I asked her to bend her mind towards modern
> problems and life as it is today. I am sure we shall get something
> valuable from this girl.[35]

The first script which Elaine handed to Wilson was *Eleven Plus*, a
look at contemporary education. It more than justified Wilson's
confidence: one reader through the script 'right on the ball' and
'jolly interesting' and that it ought to make an ideal television
drama.[36] Wilson wrote to Elaine just before Christmas, 1955, conveying the news. *Eleven Plus* was not, however, broadcast until
January 1957. The lengthy delay was due in large part to Elaine's
initial lack of knowledge and understanding of how television
worked. Until 1956 Elaine did not own a television set and so was
writing in the dark, learning as she went along and responding to
comments on her initial failures and rejections as best she could.
With encouragement from sympathetic producers like Wilson and
Douglas Allen, who guided her towards a more professional model
of television scriptwriting, Elaine was quickly able to move beyond
her apprenticeship. Allen wrote the following set of notes after
meeting with Elaine at television centre early in 1956, to reason to
himself the underlying flaws in the scripts Elaine was producing.

She certainly is very intelligent and has a flare for writing but is technically very inexperienced. She admitted that she had practically never watched TV until she bought a set a few weeks ago on the proceeds of her winning play. Miss Morgan says that she has now made all the alterations that Donald Wilson indicated to her. But there are still a few grave "howlers" such as fading out on the same artists at the end of one scene, who open the next, in a different set. She also makes much too much use of film montages, etc. With her limited experience, though, she admitted that some of these could be cut. She also has a habit of using sound effects and voices of people "off". The characterisation is quite good...

Eleven Plus underwent months of scrutiny and revision and moved from being a nationally produced programme to one made in Cardiff.[37] In the end, these changes resulted in a programme warmly received by critics and audiences. Writing in the popular Sunday paper, *The People*, for example, critic Gilbert Harding was 'full of congratulations' for Elaine and admiration for the BBC 'for their courage in putting on a play which questioned, quite openly, the effect of television on young children'.[38] Likewise, one viewer in a letter to *Western Mail* praised Elaine's willingness to tackle the growing prioritisation of science and mathematics over arts and culture:

> The most important truth was expressed by Iestyn Pugh [one of the characters] that we seem proud of our lack of talent for music, and yet ashamed for our lack of talent for mathematics. I hope Elaine Morgan will present a sequel in the near future, depicting how educational snobbery is implanted by teachers in the infant department, and not by parents.[39]

The next play which Elaine submitted, which was broadcast first, ironically, was *Without Vision*, a comedy about the disruptive arrival of television in a working-class home. The script arrived in Wilson's office in March 1956. He thought it 'an advance, technically, on Eleven Plus' and it proceeded to the production stage in June with relatively little difficulty.[40] Critical reception following broadcast in July 1956 was mostly positive. Writing in the *Liverpool Echo*, one journalist confessed 'for a long time I have waited for somebody to write a really amusing play about the impact of television on the fireside circle' ... Without Vision went a good way towards satisfying my requirements.... it doubtless gave many a viewer a sly dig in the ribs.'[41] John Lyne, in the *Western Mail,* however, thought the otherwise interesting idea had missed its moment. It would have been 'topical', he wrote, 'during the Wenvoe honeymoon period' eighteen months earlier, 'now its messages seems slightly fantastic'.[42] This was an unfair comment given only one in three households in Britain actually owned a television set in 1956 – a decade later it was nearly ninety per cent.

The third play which Elaine wrote or revised in the first half of 1956 never made it to screen in its original form, despite being regarded as something which 'ought to hit the nail on the head'.[43] Initially called 'Grey Enigma', at its heart was a story about Stonehenge – Elaine had taken up the idea when she was told in the autumn of 1955 about R.J.C. Atkinson's forthcoming, landmark study of the monument – it was to be published by Hamish Hamilton in 1956.[44] The lead character of the play was Alec, a twenty six year old archaeology graduate from Scotland who is working in a 'respectable white collar job' in a south of England museum. As a character, he was to be 'very serious, logical, hard-headed, intellectual conceited and socially uncertain', and engaged to Daphne a librarian two years his senior. Elaine picks up the story:

[Alec] has to go to a WEA class in archaeology which he tutors weekly in the back room of a pub in a village on the edge of Salisbury Plain. The class is small, but loyally indignant with Sir Basil [Wainwright]; the class secretary, Briggs, a left-wing blacksmith, stays on with him after the class, and intoxicates him with deceptively strong local cider and assures him that he has been victimised. On the pub's tv set "Panorama" is interviewing members of an international conference of archaeologists meeting in London and hoping to put in some field work in Britain. Grette, a young braided blonde from Denmark, gives a studio demonstration with her stone-age axe that the only way to prove what happened thousands of years ago is to do it again.

Grette and Alec were written in such a way as to fulfil Elaine's desire to write 'something in the Ealing tradition' and the plot wheeled towards a boy-meets-girl love story which also answered questions about how Stonehenge was erected.[45]

Unfortunately for Elaine, the character of Sir Basil Wainwright ran much too close to the real-life personality of Sir Mortimer Wheeler, formerly the director of the National Museum of Wales and at the time a popular figure – and most frequent guest – on the BBC's quiz show *Animal, Vegetable, Mineral?* presented by Glyn Daniel. Wheeler was sent the script of 'Grey Enigma' with a view to getting his approval of the Wainwright character. Although Wheeler did not, in the end, raise objections to Elaine's pen portrait, thinking the character 'so different to his own that no one will imagine that it could be meant for him'[46], the proposed programme ran into delays made necessary as producers dealt with Elaine's complex demands – seven main sets, nine minor sets, and a cast of thirty seven speaking parts and thirty non-speaking parts.[47] Unsurprisingly, it dropped off the schedule, re-appearing in May 1957 with a new title: *Do It Yourself.*[48] In its place came a drama-documentary about the Family Service Units, *F.S.U.*, an early attempt at blending fictional licence with true-to-life themes. The programme was set in and around a unit in Kensington and explored its work through the eyes of a young worker, Sheila Hutton. For veracity, the actors (in particular Silvia Herklots, who took on the lead role) were sent to live at the real-life Kensington-Paddington Family Service Unit, to 'watch the work and absorb the atmosphere'.[49] External shots were likewise filmed nearby, and Elaine spent time at the unit, herself, despite the difficulties of distance and her own familial responsibilities, learning about and researching cases that had occurred. These found their way, albeit in fictional form, into the script.

Programme makers of the late-1950s were increasingly enthusiastic about the drama documentary as a format, but neither Elaine (who had resisted attempts to turn *Eleven Plus* into a drama-documentary) nor newspaper critics were so sure: 'The BBC devotes an hour of its peak viewing time to another dramatized documentary with the unimaginative title of FSU', opined the *Shields Daily News*.[50] J.C. Griffith Jones writing in the *Western Mail* was no more excited than his northern counterpart had been, noting that 'The BBC has developed a pattern for dramatizing human problems, and Mrs Morgan's talent had to be fitted into the groove. The result did credit to her versatility, but she, like the viewers, was trapped in the maze that divides convincing truth from speculating fiction'.[51] Griffith Jones, a long-standing journalist, and radio broadcaster in his own right, further pondered the relationship between dramatic licence and truth, the freedom of a scriptwriter's pen and the interference of producers, asking readers of the *Western Mail*:

> Are our television producers going to be caught in the snare which has tripped up their colleagues in sound for too long, the snare and delusion of fact masquerading as fiction? Mrs Elaine Morgan,

the erudite South Wales writer who has won her way into the top class of television playwrights in a remarkably short time, is the latest victim of this fetish. I will risk a guess that such an intelligent and perceptive writer as Mrs Morgan would not have fictionalised the story of that humane experiment in voluntary social service, the FSU (Family Service Units), if her pen had been allowed to run free.

This was not the sense behind the scenes, however – the idea of a 'dramatised documentary' had been Elaine's from the outset, although the programme's eventual title 'F.S.U.' was applied by producers.[52] Writing to the producer John Elliot, in early June 1956, she proposed a programme 'showing the kinds of lives lived by the submerged fiftieth today – and showing women demonstrating the kind of patience and courage that the Salvation Army demanded of them in Major Barbara's day'.[53] The two met shortly afterwards: Elaine successfully dissuaded Elliot from turning Eleven Plus into a drama-documentary, Elliot, in turn, convinced Elaine that she should write something about the family service units in the format. In her correspondence, Elaine explained that she had already subscribed to the Stepney FSU's newsletter, had arranged a meeting with one of its social workers, and had provisionally booked to discuss the topic with the FSU's national secretary, David John, 'if you (the BBC) decide to go ahead'.[54] She similarly sought out Douglas Woodhouse, a researcher based at the London School of Economics, whose work on the FSU was later integrated into Albert Philip's 1963 study Family Failure.[55]

By September 1956, Elaine's work on the documentary was in full swing and she sent in a treatment describing a range of characters and settings: three quite different families (one English, one Irish, and one composed of immigrants from Europe), FSU field-workers including the lead character Sheila, and an 'outsider' called

Brian, a politically-radical medical student from Oxford who thinks the FSU a load of upper class do-goodery designed simply to interfere in working-class lives.[56] Elaine's own views were carefully disguised in the final programme, but clear in a letter she sent to John Elliot in late October, as she resisted the urge of the BBC to make Sheila working-class rather than middle-class:

> I can't make her non-U like the families. The hard fact is, working class people never go in for that kind of thing – I only met one even conceivably in that category. The whole point is that she knows she is different, and feels guilty about the difference and the reasons for it, and at bottom is a little bit scared of them... Get a stock girl with a nice stubborn face – but her accent his cultured. There's no getting around that it's her first hurdle ... they have voices like duchesses, those Quaker helpers.
> ...This theory that everybody of 22 is a crazy mixed-up kid is the great literary fallacy of the twentieth century, dreamed up by somebody whose mother was frightened by Patience Strong.[57]

Elaine's follow up drama-documentary, broadcast in March 1958, drew attention to impact of opencast coal mining and what happened when opposition was rallied by a prominent local figure – in this instance, the district councillor. *Black Furrow* was made with the (eventual acquiescence and) support of the National Coal Board and its Welsh setting allowed Elaine to research without having to travel back and forth to London. 'Domestically', she confessed after the broadcast of *F.S.U*, 'it's a lot simpler to sit by the fire and dream up fiction'. It had not been the first choice of topic – Elaine had wished to write about old age pensioners, and her colleagues had encouraged her to think about local government corruption. Neither suited: the former because it had been taken by another scriptwriter, the latter because, as Elaine explained:

As a theme it's always anti-Labour, because it's always most hotly rumoured in areas where the councillors have for years been either out of work or much worse paid than the people they appoint. I don't know how much there really is, nor how anyone would go about finding out. Obviously nobody would talk. If I concluded there was none, people would call it a whitewash; it I concluded there was a good deal, people would say I'd dug up authentic dirt via my husband who is Vice Chairman of the party [in Aberdare]; there'd be an awful stink, the Tories would rejoice, and Morien would probably be out on his ear. It would need to be done by a fearless Liberal living at least 150 miles away from the area concerned.[58]

As a topic, corruption, or at least abuse of an elected position, found its way into the writings of Gwyn Thomas – in his novel *A Point of Order* (1956) and his radio play 'The Alderman' (1966) – Kingsley Amis, in *That Uncertain Feeling* (1955), and in Glyn Jones's 1960 novel *The Learning Lark*. These may well have motivated interest on the part of BBC producers, but Elaine stuck to her position. *Black Furrow*, with its attendant links to life in Abernant and the open-cast mine in that part of Aberdare, emerged as a compromise. But even this compromise almost came unstuck when producers expressed a degree of concern that they would be broadcasting two 'disaster' documentaries set in Wales featuring an apparently uncaring external force imposing its will on the locals. The other setting: Tryweryn. Elaine replied:

This subject won't overlap Tryweryn at all. In that the victims will be simple country folk, the agitators Welsh Nationalists, and the "oppressors" Liverpool Corporation with quite a good humanitarian case of their own; after all Lancashire must drink, and even wash. In ours the people will all be quite different. It will just be a general goaded growl of a populace pushed around too long; tough and articulate; Labour and the Tories both a bit leery of giving leadership to the discontent and one or two cranks playing along with it; the Socialists' agonising reappraisal of their pet nationalised industry...[59]

* * *

By the spring of 1958, Elaine was highly regarded as a scriptwriter for radio and most especially television. She was in demand for profiles in women's magazines such as *Modern Woman* – much to her own amusement – and was lauded by the press in Wales as the 'most successful TV drama and feature writer' of Welsh origin.[60] But Elaine's own modesty, and sometimes her own determination to present as a mother first and foremost, allowed her talents and professionalism to be moderated into the soubriquet 'housewife-dramatist', which gave off more than a whiff of amateurism.[61] Some of this was Elaine's own fault: as she told the *Western Mail*, motherhood was her profession and writing was, to a large extent, merely a hobby. 'It brings in some of the excitement of show business', she said, 'without interfering with the main job'.[62] As late as the publicity runs for *Descent of Woman* in the early 1970s, by which time Elaine had been writing professionally for twenty years, she was still labelled as the 'housewife' who became a 'bestselling authoress'.[63] This has meant, in the long term, a considerable undervaluing of Elaine's importance in the development of postwar television; put simply she was one of the BBC's pre-eminent Welsh writers, certainly its most lauded Welsh woman, one who had worked on contract for the corporation since 1956.

Elaine's modesty and the false impression given of her career is to be regretted. For she was a pioneer as a television scriptwriter. There were few women working in senior roles anywhere in the

BBC in the 1950s. The Talks Department had just five women staff members out of more than forty – two producers, two production assistants, and the assistant Head of Department, Grace Wyndham Goldie.[64] In the 1960s, opportunities for women sharply declined, such that by the 1970s women were regarded as lacking ability and authority, and men in senior positions could safely express sexist views without any fear of challenge. The head of light entertainment in the early 1970s, for example, did not 'like to see trousered girls charging about the studio in a sexless way'.[65] Others expressed concerns that women would not be able to keep up with 'necessary' alcohol consumption at meetings and lunches and that 'the producer occasionally has to invite a Ken Dodd to lunch... a female producer would find this difficult'.[66] Elaine's own research on women's involvement in television, published in 1979, showed that just ten per cent of scripted output on the BBC and ITV in the previous year had been by women. A situation which could hardly be 'explained away', she concluded, by the notion that 'men are ten times more effective at handling words, creating characters, or inventing plots'.[67]

There is an irony here, which deserves identification and correction. By 1960, the year Elaine's first major serial, *A Matter of Degree*, was broadcast, her work had appeared on television nine times together with dozens of radio contributions for domestic and overseas audiences. In an era when women's writing was largely restricted to domestic matters or aimed at children, and often penned by children's novelists such as Dora Broome, Elaine was one of the first to break through into other areas of writing especially serious drama and drama-documentary. But she is rarely remembered for the significance of that advance, or for the fact that it came before those who have subsequently gained much greater fame as 'isolated *female* voice[s] in a wave of 1950s new writing', not least the playwright Shelagh Delaney.[68] Whilst Delaney's breakthrough reputation rests on her play *A Taste of Honey*, its debut on the London stage in May 1958 came a few weeks *after* Elaine's first true play, *The Waiting Room*, which was set late at night in Paddington Station, was broadcast on BBC television. *A Taste of Honey* made its reputation as part of the kitchen sink dramas of the 1950s which gave voice to the realities of post-war working-class life. *The Waiting Room* had these themes in abundance, too, featuring as its main characters an Irish woman feeling her husband, a young Welsh woman running away from home, and a recent West Indian immigrant who was escaping her abusive partner. J.C. Griffiths Jones, writing in the *Western Mail*, enthused about Elaine's 'pulsating human drama'.[69]

Kitchen sink realism was never really associated with Elaine's work despite her clear synergy – although she was writing for television, of course, whereas the mainstay of the kitchen sinks (John Osborne at their head) wrote for the theatre.[70] Such was the resonance between Elaine's work in this period and the kitchen sink dramatists that in 1964 – when she first took part in *Any Questions?* – Elaine moved to defend the genre against accusations it was unserious and just about sex and provocative titillation:

I've got this much to say for the dramatists: I think the writers of those plays are deadly serious people and trying to put over a message, whether you like the message or not. There's also this technical problem, that if you cannot hold your audience in the first five minutes of the play, they've switched over to ITV, and therefore you've got to put something that holds them in the first five minutes. Now then, I've written about twenty plays; I only ever wrote one which started with a woman in her petticoat pulling on a stocking, and that got the highest rating of the week apart from one American show, and I have never hit that level since.[71]

She continued:

> I'm seriously claiming, yes, that people writing these plays, mostly they are young men and they're trying to come to terms with the problem of sex, and the whole moral atmosphere has gone so much to pieces that they don't know where to start from, they're … it is the think that's most on their minds, they're most worried about it, and they're trying to work it out in fiction, and the reason that they haven't got an end, a beginning, a middle, and an end, is that they don't know what to think themselves, partly, partly they're trying to put over a message and say life is pointless, life is dreary, life is depressing – they haven't got a message for you, they haven't got anything positive. It may be – it may be very unfortunate, but I don't think they're being frivolous – I think it might be better if they were. I think they'd be more capable of being frivolous if they'd made up their own minds about it.

Unbeknown to the audience in Plymouth that evening, Elaine had had plenty of experience of men having an uncertain attitude towards sex – not least from Morien. Within a couple of years of working for the BBC, Elaine had raised enough money to meet the thousand pounds deposit that he had insisted upon before the couple tried for a third child. To accelerate her income, Elaine had taken on teaching jobs in addition to writing, re-joining the WEA as a tutor in 1954 – her classes were in Aberaman, Aberdare, and Troedyrhiw, together with appearances on the guest lecture circuit around the valleys.[72] Then, in the autumn of 1955, she took on a job as a lecturer at Aberdare College of Further Education where she taught history, geography, arithmetic, English, and social studies, all on an hourly paid contract. 'It is gruelling' she wrote in a letter to the Cooperative Correspondence Club, 'I went to bed one night with a paper-wrapped toffee and was asleep before I could unwrap it!' So much for opportunities to entice Morien into natural conception; and so much for the idea, reiterated in her memoir, that she was a 'wife and mother, [with] two lovely children, [and an] inexpensive little hobby' who could earn the thousand pounds as deposit for a third child 'without going out of the house'. Elaine may have wanted to be 'a writer, not a teacher' but she had little choice other than to maintain both aspects of her burgeoning career in order to fulfil her ambitions as a mother.

The practicalities of pregnancy as Elaine approached her forties were increasingly evident. She continued to confide her worries and frustrations in her letters to the women of the Co-operative Correspondence Club but with each passing year, and with Morien's intransigence, it became apparent that she was unlikely to conceive naturally. 'I did at one point consult a doctor', Elaine reflected later, 'he mentioned my age ... some stuff called Fertilol'. This was made from wheat germ and was intended to increase the presence of Vitamin E in the body. It had been issued to pregnant women – and those hoping to become pregnant – for decades but in Elaine's case it was 'no good'.[73] In an oblique letter to Donald Wilson, written in October 1957, Elaine revealed that she had miscarried two months into a pregnancy. 'I'm forbidden to try again for some months', she wrote.[74] Instead, Elaine and Morien began to discuss the possibility of adoption, fully aware that 'forty ... is considered a watershed when it comes to adopting. They won't look at you. I was by then thirty-seven'. Several organisations were approached, including Christian charities and Glamorgan County Council, to varying levels of success – and sadness. The first child Elaine and Morien were to adopt, a baby girl, died shortly before coming to live them. After a miscarriage and a sudden infant death, 'the fight had finally gone out of me, it was all over'.

As so often, given Morien's relative disinterest, Elaine expressed much of her anguish in her letters to the Cooperative Correspondence Club, and it was from this source that she received a second chance at adoption. Counsel came from Rose Hacker (1906-2008), 'Elektra' to club members, who worked for the Marriage Guidance Council as a relationship advisor and was later elected to London County Council.[75] It was Rose Hacker who, in 1960, linked Elaine and Morien to a schoolgirl who was looking to give up her baby son for adoption. 'I shot up to London like a greyhound out of the slips', Elaine recalled. Rose Hacker accompanied Elaine to the home from where the baby was to be collected and provided her with support and advice through the legal process involved in formally adopting the child. He was named Morien Huw Morgan, known to all as Huw. Although Elaine had not achieved her dream of being mother to a little girl, Huw's arrival helped to revitalise life with Morien. The process of adoption had not been an easy one and had placed considerable strain on relations between Elaine and her husband. Little wonder that, as she was to put it, 'I have never had the slightest cause to regret taking [Huw] on, and plenty of reasons to feel glad that I did'.

This unhappy period of Elaine's domestic life saw her take on more and more public responsibilities, not least in the campaign against nuclear armaments proliferation. It was a stance shared with Morien, who took the lead in organising Aberdare's substantial Ban-the-Bomb Week in 1958 and served as chair of the Aberdare and Mountain Ash Ban-the-Bomb Committee. However, it was Elaine rather than Morien who took a seat on the Welsh National Council of CND. She spoke at the launch of the Council in October 1958, for example, alongside George Thomas MP and Dick Beamish of the South Wales Area of the NUM.[76] Three years later, she marched at the head of the first All-Wales Nuclear Disar-

mament Rally, held in Aberystwyth, and took her place on the plat-
form alongside other members of the Welsh National Council.
These included Emrys Roberts the organising secretary of Plaid
Cymru, who had previously been the Council's secretary, the
Quaker John Dennithorne of the Dowlais Settlement, and the
Bishop of Llandaff, Glyn Simon. Amongst the two thousand others
who marched that day were the actress Sian Phillips, the composer
Grace Williams, the poet T.E. Nicholas, and the maverick Merthyr
Tydfil MP, S.O. Davies, as well as students, communists, trade union-
ists, CND branch members from across Wales, and various branches
of the Labour Party and Plaid Cymru.

Through Elaine and Morien's enterprise, the Ban-the-Bomb
Week held in Aberdare in September 1958 was one of the largest
in the country.[77] It featured church services; a youth night; a Brains
Trust featuring Elaine and the writer and broadcaster Gwyn
Thomas; a specially-commissioned play; and a public meeting
addressed by historian A.J.P. Taylor (who later served as the historical consultant for Elaine's adaptation of the life of David Lloyd
George) and the South Wales NUM President Will Paynter.[78] Taylor
was, by then, amongst the most prominent of CND's national cam-
paigners and a member of the organisation's executive committee.
He was indicative of the largely middle-class orientation of anti-
nuclear protest in the 1950s and 1960s and joined a campaign
group which included the editor of the New Statesman, Kingsley
Martin, in whose flat CND was tentatively formed, and Bertrand
Russell who served as its chair.[79] For a period in the 1970s, clearly
proud of the fact, Elaine made much in her professional biography
of once sharing a platform with Russell in Cardiff. This followed
her successful attempt to bring traffic in the city to a standstill when
she sat down in the middle of Queen Street – direct action long
remembered by those who witnessed it.[80]

CND activism provided the inspiration both for Elaine's 1962 series 'Barbara in Black' and for her, at the time, controversial 1963 drama *Licence to Murder*. Her first full play for the stage, it was produced by the acclaimed Michael Codron and Donald Albery and performed, albeit to a limited and relatively unsuccessful run of five nights, at the Vaudeville Theatre in London. *Licence to Murder* pondered the consequences of the nuclear paranoia and was set in an American courtroom where a fallout-shelter owner has been put on trial for killing an intruder during a practice drill for a nuclear attack. After its initial performance, Elaine's play enjoyed a far more successful second life in repertory theatre and was performed across the country, including at the Grand Theatre in Swansea in July 1964.[81] One reviewer, responding to a production at the Belgrade Theatre in Coventry, drew obvious connections with contemporary television courtroom drama such as *Perry Mason*.[82] Success in regional theatre encouraged a television adaptation which appeared on ITV – a rare venture away from the BBC – as part of its Armchair Mystery Theatre season in May 1965, directed by Basil Coleman. Reception was somewhat mixed, with reviews splitting along a conventional left-right political spectrum. Clive Barnes of the *Daily Express* complained, for instance, that 'all you learned was never go visiting American fallout shelters during a practice alert'.[83]

Yet, akin to the play's reception in provincial theatres in Britain, *Licence to Murder* was received rather better elsewhere in Europe. Perhaps because of the underlying politics of Elaine's writing, and in the context of a growing anti-nuclear campaign across the continent, the play was readily adapted for television and radio audiences on both sides of the Iron Curtain. In March 1966, the play was screened on West German television as *Kein Freibrief für Mord*, directed by Karl-Heinz Bieber and produced by the

Munich-based Elan-Film Gierke and Company. The same production was shown on East German television the following year. An Austrian adaptation, using the same script translation but a different cast, was produced by the Vienna bureau of state broadcaster ORF in November 1966. Likewise, the availability of the script in German encouraged further transmissions in Eastern Europe, such as the 1977 Polish adaptation directed by Wojciech Marczewski. Elaine was hardly alone in having her work translated into a variety of European languages, nor the only Welsh writer of this period whose appeal crossed the continent of Europe, both were traits she shared with Gwyn Thomas; but whereas her fame in the West later rested on her scientific writing, rather than her work for television and radio, her renown in Eastern Europe was almost entirely political and linked to her creative writing.

But it was not politics which propelled Elaine's career into its golden age so much as a return to student life at Oxford. In March 1960, *The Stage* published an advertisement for two young actresses to star in a forthcoming serial to be penned by Elaine Morgan. 'They must be either Welsh or possess a convincing Welsh accent', the advert stated, 'must be about 18 or look that age and, roughly 5ft 3 ins tall'.[84] The two characters were to be the Powell sisters, Doreen and Mavis. One destined for university, the other a life at home in the South Wales Valleys. It was a theme which Elaine had resisted for some time. Perhaps because the unhappy circumstances of marriage had brought back memories of Drummond Allison and her lost love. Perhaps because Elaine really did believe she lacked the talent to write such a programme. Even when *A Matter of Degree* was broadcast in the early summer of 1960, Elaine maintained that it was not an autobiographical work. The critics did not entirely believe her. All the same, they were universal in their praise for a writer whose career, in the space of a mere five years, had gone from the disaster of *Mirror, Mirror* to being the very reason that, in the words of the *Liverpool Echo*, 'in this television age ... they [the Welsh] have a definite claim to a connection with good TV drama'.[85]

FOUR
THEY CAN'T TAKE
IT FROM YOU

A Matter of Degree had its origins in a discussion over lunch in London in February 1957 between Elaine, Donald Wilson, and the *Daily Mail*'s television critic, Peter Black. Intrigued by Elaine's life story and impressed by her work, Black had pressed Wilson for a meeting so that he could find out more. In his columns, Black painted Elaine as 'redoubtable' and a 'socially-conscious TV dramatist' whose real skill lay in recognising that 'the drama which really absorbs people does not lie in murder and adultery, but in the seeming commonplaces of ordinary life'.[1] She was, in his view, the only contemporary writer for television to have grasped that moral. Once the idea of writing about Oxford had come into view, Donald Wilson kept prodding Elaine to make it her priority.[2] Although interested in the idea, Elaine resisted for quite a while, explaining to Wilson that 'I think the blockage has been that all through my first term, which would be the most significant time to set the play in, my father was dying, and died at Christmas; it is hard for me to think of it without that colouring it'.[3] For a year the idea lay dormant, a hiatus which Elaine had insisted upon whilst she completed her other projects for 1957. She picked it back up again in February 1958, writing to Donald Wilson expressing second thoughts.

Very sorry to sound coy about this, but I really don't feel ripe to tackle it, and I still think to do it as a women's college interior would be too cramping. I can just glimpse glorious possibilities in doing an Amis with it, substituting Lucky Jane for Lucky Jim and grey atone for red brick; but it might, equally, prove a glorious flop. There are one or two sitting targets for this treatment – e.g. the crusty "leftwing" dons who still resent and affect to ignore the presence of women students; but by and large it's a hell of a place to try and take the micky out of because the fit target for satire is pettiness of various kinds and I don't think Oxford is a petty place.[4]

In his marginalia to Elaine's letter, Wilson rejected the idea of tacking the mickey and instead noted the idea of the piece should be a view of Oxford, its life and people, as seen 'through the eyes of a young woman from a Welsh valley'. In his reply to Elaine, he added 'you say yourself Oxford is not a bad place. I imagine you would not have aspired to go there if you had thought so in the first place'.[5] She stalled once again, this time proposing 'an objective sort of programme on the Freemasons'.[6] For months the idea swirled around the BBC machine with Elaine left to go it alone with her research – the idea eventually fizzled out with little interest shown in it either by BBC producers or the masons themselves. In danger of not meeting the terms of her contract, Elaine reluctantly turned back to Oxford, proposing a quasi-sequel to Emlyn Williams's *The Corn is Green*.[7] In her initial treatment, Elaine called what was intended to be a single episode teleplay, 'They Can't Take It From You'. Many of the final elements were there from outset: the clear differences between Doreen and Mavis and the disorientation of the former as soon as she arrives at Oxford. But in her third term she meets Julian, an ex-public schoolboy and rebel who is 'leftish in a woolly, literary, apocalyptic sort of way. Brecht and Behan and Beckett are his prophets'.[8]

The autobiographical detail was much more overt in the treatment than in the final script, not least in Doreen's habit of joining various clubs which 'entail arguing and getting things done rather than making the kind of small-talk she has never learned'. Although it is not named directly, this was clearly a reference to Elaine's own past in the Democratic Socialist Club. After discussing the treatment with Michael Barry, Donald Wilson wrote back to Elaine offering a six-part serial, rather than a single episode play. 'We both feel', he explained, 'that three hours screen-time will give you a chance of telling us more about the Powell family'.[9] Cock-a-hoop as well as daunted at the prospect of writing multi-part serials, rather than just one offs, Elaine told Wilson that

> I was going to do Oxford from memory, but if we're going to have
> time to get close to it I must go up and take another look, espe-
> cially at the undergraduates ... I've got one or two contacts there,
> like that Dennis Potter lad, I met him before Christopher Mayhew
> made such a hit with him, and he will help in any way he can.[10]

To understand how to write a serial, Elaine was sent − on her request − the scripts for *Champion Road* which had been broadcast on BBC television in September and October 1958. The key differ-ence between Elaine's proposal and her model was that the latter was based on a 1948 novel by Frank Tilsley. Nevertheless, Elaine had requested the scripts in order to 'study the anatomy of a good serial ... I feel it might give me a clearer idea of just how to go about it'.[11] Elaine's outline arrived at the BBC in January 1959 and was read by both Donald Wilson and Michael Barry. Her proposal was pioneering in a number of ways: delivering a view of Oxford life decades ahead of more famous series like *Brideshead Revisited* (1981) and *Porterhouse Blue* (1987), both adaptations of well-known novels, as well as introducing overtly homosexual characters at a time, just a couple of years after the publication of the 1957

Wolfenden Report, when these had almost never been on television before. One scene in part three was to include 'a "queer" schoolmaster and a bitchy woman of uncertain age' who have somehow gate-crashed an undergraduate party hosted by Julian. In his letter to Elaine, Wilson declared the outline to be 'splendid' but told her that Michael Barry had requested she 'Go easy on the Queers'.[12] There was, however, no attempt to prevent Elaine from dealing with the subject – the BBC were more nervous about another part of the script, as Wilson explained. 'Thank you very much for part 5, which I think is fine', he wrote, 'I am afraid not even Lil can get away with "bugger" on the television screen'.[13]

As Elaine progressed with writing the scripts, sending them in for comment at regular intervals during the spring of 1959, the comments made by Wilson and Barry focused in on the portrayal of Oxford as a discursive rather than active 'get on with it' environment. Donald Wilson summarised part four's plot as 'the homespun Welsh getting on with their sex life while Oxford talks about it!'[14] He elaborated the observation in a letter to Elaine, telling her that 'Michael and I are both mad about' the distinction between the active Welsh full of life and the chatty Oxonians who seemed to have no other purpose.[15] Wilson was convinced that 'we have got something quite original here – something that has never been done before'.[16] By the end of 1959, 'They Can't Take It From You' had become 'The Ladder', a still somewhat imperfect title for the serial as a whole, and was soon replaced with a second alternative 'When You Come Back' – which itself had been originally the title of part two.[17] Only at last minute, with the pressure of advertising in the *Radio Times* and advance notices for the newspapers, did the serial gain its final title *A Matter of Degree*. Some of the cast had their own nickname: 'One Degree Under'.[18]

As written and as broadcast, *A Matter of Degree* revealed a

striking autobiographical narrative. The series was located in a fictionalised South Walian town, albeit one in such close proximity
to the St Gwynno Forestry that it could only have been Pontypridd. The backdrop to the story provided one element of Elaine's
mirror image, the character of Doreen Powell, the bookish and
class-aware protagonist, another one that was undoubtedly compelling as a portrait of the dislocation caused by going up to Oxford
from the South Wales Valleys. In her initial drafts, Elaine sent Doreen
from the coalfield to St Margaret's College, Oxford: a very thin disguise for Lady Margaret Hall. During the revision stage ahead of
filming, however, Elaine decided to adopt the more oblique St
Mary's College – itself associated with both Oriel College and New
College. The absence of a more thorough reworking of the setting,
however, meant that even this new name did little to disguise its
obvious inspiration. The key revelatory scene, laying out a version
of Elaine's private experiences of Oxford, occurred in part two and
took place in the rooms of Doreen's bourgeois friend, Rosamund:

Doreen: I think it was that fresher's party that got me down most,
the first week, wasn't it? All those girls standing about in that huge
room, balancing those silly little coffee cups. I couldn't understand
why we couldn't sit down, I mean, and relax.... I knew I was having
kittens all the time, because I never knew when I'd put my foot in
it next. The really stupid thing is, the only thing I did have in
common with them was banned. I can't talk travel, I can't talk theatres, I can't talk hockey and lacrosse. I can't ask 'are you related to
the Berkshire Jones?' I could have talked like a torrent about books,
but that's taboo. That's talking shop.

Rosamund: Then what have we been doing for the last two hours?

Doreen: (BLISSFUL) Ah, tonight, yes. The first time, though.

Rosamund: Oh, come. I'm sure I heard Deborah trying to talk books to you at dinner last night!

Doreen: What? Oh that! Did you hear it?

Rosamund: It was the funniest thing I've heard for years!

Doreen: She must have thought I was raving mad! But when she said Beatrice Potter, I naturally thought she meant Sidney Webb's wife. I'd never even heard of the Flopsy Bunnies.

Rosamund: No? What did you cut your teeth on?

Doreen: Beryl the Peril... Dennis the Menace...

The hints in Elaine's autobiography suggest that, despite her protestations to the contrary, Doreen Powell was indeed an authorial cipher. 'I was a bit obtuse', Elaine wrote. 'Some of the things I said and did may well have – make that "must have" – set their teeth on edge … The signals they used to convey those things to one another – slight alterations to the intonation or the angle of an eyebrow – were so minimal and delicate that unless you'd been brought up to read them they were invisible'. Oxford did rankle, though, and Elaine's inherent South Walian-ness meant that she was able to express sympathy with the response of her near contemporaries to the same culture clash:

Doreen: You know, this is what I'd read about Oxford. That boy in the *Corn is Green*, the very first night he was talking the moon up with somebody. I thought, it's not going to happen though. It's a lie, Gwyn Thomas was nearer the mark.

Rosamund: Where?

Doreen: Oh, one of his cracks. I forget who told me now. Someone said to him when he'd been up here a bit, 'If you feel like that about it Thomas, what are you doing here anyway?' He said, 'I got on the wrong bus at Bargoed'. I thought, I'm on the wrong bus too.

Rosamund: Oh, I don't think so. I think whatever happened, one would regret not having been here.

Given the closer proximity of Doreen Powell's sentiments to those of Gwyn Thomas, who hated Oxford, or Emlyn Williams, who experienced a breakdown there, this must be nearer the truth of much of Elaine's time at Oxford than the later expressions of love and enjoyment, which were themselves bound up with her relationship with Drummond Allison. Both women coped by being active – almost hyper-active – in student societies and politics. As Doreen explains to Rosamund, 'I seem to have got involved in a lot of things, somehow. The Labour Club, play reading do's, and subediting the *Phoenix*'.

The honesty on display in *A Matter of Degree* did not cover personal feelings, and the clash of classes and cultures, alone. Elaine could hardly avoid the contemporary retreat of the coal mining industry and the artificial return of forests to the hillsides and mountaintops of South Wales. The St Gwynno Forestry, first planted in 1937, was an important phase of the landscape restoration of the valleys north of Pontypridd and was the setting for Doreen's reunion with her erstwhile boyfriend, Glyn Morris. The latter was working for the Forestry Commission as a ranger and challenged Doreen's singular perspective on mining and the future of South Wales.

Glyn: People always talk as if this job was something archaic. If anything's *Gone With the Wind*, it's that down there, the mining. When my father started you could see fourteen pits from here, all working full blast. Now there's two. In twenty years it'll all be over, and nothing left but a squalid mess it's nobody's business to tidy up, and a little town full of old age pensioners.

Doreen: I don't believe it, they'll find another use for coal.

Glyn: Why should they?

Doreen: Because of the miners, of course.

Glyn: All the miners need is work to last their own lives out. None of them wants to send his sons underground. Who in his senses would want to send anybody there?

Doreen: Whose side are you on? It's better than the dole, isn't it?

Glyn: ... It's not a fit place for anyone to work. Finish with it. Find them something decent to do.

Doreen: Well, I think it's for the miners to decide. It's they'll be affected by it.

Glyn: We'll all be affected. You and me and everybody. You can't have a great Colossus like that having death rattles in your back yard and go on as if nothing was happening.

This was a theme which Elaine had previously explored in her study of opencast mining, *Black Furrow*, in 1958. Then, in Dave Berry's words, she had given 'vent to her own anger over opencast mining pollution' near her home in Abernant.[19] She would return to the effects of mining in 'Dust', an episode of *Dr Finlay's* Casebook broadcast in December 1970. Herein were prototypes (and forms) of the emerging environmental themes of Anglo-Welsh literature evident in the 1950s and 1960s. Gwyn Thomas had explored the theme in his novel *Point of Order* and in subsequent radio plays including 'The Alderman'. Ron Berry's 1968 novel *Flame and Slag*, one of the most important contributions, expressed similar sentiments to those found in Elaine's television writing – albeit, in his case, charged with post-Aberfan outrage.[20]

Reviewers took less interest in the environmental considerations of the serial than the educational implications. At the end of part six, Doreen Powell made up her mind to end her degree early and return home to Wales to live a life of domesticity. That was, of course, a fate which Elaine had herself avoided because of the determination of her mother to make the sacrifices necessary to finish. It is difficult not to see, with hindsight, Doreen Powell's decision to leave as a counterfactual exploration of Elaine's own life chances. But was the series successful in its conclusion? One otherwise supportive critic, writing in the *Liverpool Echo*, thought that it was not. They wrote:

> as the last scene faded away I could imagine the spluttering indignation of many viewers at that girl, on whom the State had spent so much money, calmly leaving Oxford after two years without wanting a degree. I could also imagine Welsh girls following in "Taffy's" footsteps having a slightly more difficult time in persuading parents to let them attend university after last night's termination of "Taffy's" career.[21]

The Birmingham Daily Post was more scathing and unsympathetic: the series, in its view, was 'contrived, womanish psychosociology' and 'fizzled out into a paradoxically blank pattern'.[22] Such sentiments did not prevent a sequel, the only one of Elaine's career, which was commissioned towards the end of 1964 for broadcast on BBC Wales in the spring of 1965. It was repeated across Britain in the summer of that year. Running to two series of six episodes, *Lil* focused on the most enduring character from *A Matter of Degree*, Lil Thomas, played by the Mountain Ash-born actor Jessie Evans (1918-1983).[23] It continued the exploration of gender relations and society in the South Wales Valleys established in the earlier serial but replaced drama with situational comedy – one of the episodes was set, for instance, in the salon of a gay French hairdresser called Gabriel; and the first in the series saw Lil 'pit her wits against a soapflake salesman and her neighbour Blod'.[24] Warmly received by critics and audiences alike, the authentic Welsh voices of Elaine's characters spoke to many who watched the series, as though Lil and Blod were relatives or neighbours of their own.[25]

One of the ideas which, much to Elaine's irritation, did not get produced but which found an echo in the much later comedy programmes written by Jimmy Perry and David Croft was a take on the fifties enthusiasm for holiday camps such as Butlins and Pontins. When Elaine proposed the programme in the summer of 1959, Donald Wilson thought it a brilliant idea. 'I think', he told colleagues, 'this could be gay and good fun with Elaine behind the typewriter'. In retrospect, this proposal can only be read as a prototype of *Hi-de-Hi*, itself set in 1959, albeit one dreamt up thirty years ahead of its time. Likewise, whereas *Hi-de-Hi* was set in a fictional holiday camp in Essex, Elaine's proposal was for a holiday camp in Pwllheli in North Wales, which could only be one of those operated by Billy Butlin. Both the BBC, aside from Donald Wilson, at least, and Butlin's responded to Elaine's idea with a degree of nervousness, however, prompting yet another round of discussions and negotiations before the script was eventually cancelled. For the first time, Elaine felt angry at having been encouraged to work on a script which was not brought to screen and her agent demanded payment for the work. In the end, the unproduced script was accepted as part of her 1959-60 contract.

There was another good reason for Elaine's obvious annoyance.[26] She had found it difficult to convince Morien to travel north, even for a research trip turned holiday. So, she conspired with her neighbours, Celia and Noël Thomas, that they would go as a group, together with their children. The Thomases were schoolteachers – the latter rising to become Head of English in 1965 and then in 1977 the final headmaster of Aberdare Boys' Grammar School – and were active figures in Aberdare Labour Party. Noël served as chair of the Constituency Labour Party in the early 1960s. Unsurprisingly, he was someone whom Morien held in high regard. Thus, Elaine (together with Celia) reasoned that if Noël travelled, so would Morien. The conspirators were proven correct and they enjoyed a welcome respite in North Wales that summer. In Celia Thomas, who was part of the radical Greening-Wilson family in Aberdare and an accomplished (and later widely-published) poet, Elaine herself found a kindred spirit. A high achiever at Aberdare Girls' Grammar School, with a particular interest in literature and classics, Celia Thomas was destined, like Elaine, to study at Oxbridge (in her case, Cambridge), but unlike Elaine was forced by circumstance to turn away from that path and into primary school teaching.

With success, despite holiday camp hiccups, came the realisation that Elaine was being significantly underpaid by the BBC in comparison with other scriptwriters of her stature. By the summer of 1959, Elaine was being paid twelve hundred guineas (or £1,260 – the equivalent of just under £30,000 today) to write four television plays, a sum raised to fourteen hundred guineas towards the end of the year.[27] Just two years earlier her income was one hundred and seventy five guineas per script: exactly half.[28] A few months after the broadcast of *A Matter of Degree*, Donald Wilson intervened to propose that Elaine be paid even more. 'I am', he wrote to his colleagues, 'anxious that Mrs Morgan's fees should now be on a par with writers of equal calibre – up 'til now she has tended to be underpaid'.[29] Her new fee structure was to be four hundred and fifty guineas for a ninety-minute play – or one hundred and fifty for every thirty minutes of television broadcast. Based on four plays a year, or in 1960-61 one play and six-part serial, this would have earned Elaine the equivalent of more than £40,000 today. It was an income on a par with middle management-level jobs in the civil service and was around three times the average salary. She was, in other words, one of the highest earners living anywhere in the South Wales Valleys of the early 1960s.

Some of the uplift in income undoubtedly came from the proactive pressure on the BBC's copyright department applied by Elaine's agents – John Johnson (until 1960), Walter Jokel (from 1960 until 1962), and finally Harvey Unna (from January 1962 onwards). The latter, the only agent mentioned by Elaine in her memoir, is now most famous for his role in securing the publication of Michael Bond's Paddington Bear stories, as well as his work as a translator at the Nuremburg Trials. He had come to Britain as a refugee from Nazi Germany in the 1930s. Unna had been on course to become the youngest judge in the country but, as a middle-class Jew, the rise of the Nazis meant that his name was added to government watchlists and in the end Unna fled.[30] After the Second World War, Unna created one of the most important theatrical and literary agencies in London and came to represent many of the writers, directors, and producers, responsible for 'much of the best in postwar drama, comedy and television serials'.[31] Joining Unna's list of clients in the early 1960s was an indication of Elaine's arrival as one of the major television scriptwriters in the country.[32]

Television scriptwriting was only one aspect of Elaine's relationship with the BBC, albeit that it provided her with most
regularly contracted work. Additional income and engagement
came as a result of invitations from other departments to broadcast
or to appear as a guest, these included for overseas and domestic
audiences on the radio, appearances on programmes such as
Tonight, and, for a time, presenting the television chat show,
Crosstalk, for BBC Wales.[33] Elaine recalled 'interviewing characters
like the Welsh millionaire Julian Hodge, and Lord Chalfont, and
Gerald Navarro, the flamboyant Tory MP with the superabundant
moustache'. Her first appearance was on 23 April 1968 – the first
episode of the programme, which was intended to mark Shakespeare's birthday – and she continued until mid–October giving up
the role, apparently, because of the discomfort evidenced by Morien
– he was no fan of the domestic disturbances that regular television
presenting required. 'I knew', Elaine wrote later, 'he was wondering
where this new trajectory was likely to end up'. In the event, only
one further episode of *Crosstalk* was broadcast after Elaine's departure – in December 1968. The programme did not carry on
without her although she never again stepped in front of the television cameras as host, preferring instead to appear as guest
contributor or to maintain her distance through writing, perhaps
so as not to upset Morien any further.

A few years earlier, in 1962, the arrival of the Canadian Sydney
Newman as Head of Drama had transformed Elaine's prospects.
Newman promptly got rid of the Script Department in its then
form and Donald Wilson moved to become Head of Serials – he
retired from the BBC two years later having been an important
figure in the launch of BBC Two. The staff shuffles imposed by
Newman meant that Elaine found herself dealing with new executives and producers who, initially, were less sympathetic than

THEY CAN'T TAKE IT FROM YOU

Wilson had been. He intervened in July 1962 to encourage his colleagues to look after her. 'I have always found that the best way with Elaine', he wrote to story editor David Whitaker, 'is to get her to come up for a day to talk things over'.[34] Serendipitously, it was a different story editor, Harry Green, who provided Elaine with a route into one of her longest lasting assignments – *Dr Finlay's Casebook*. Green came from Neath and knew both Elaine and Morien, and several other Welsh writers including the Abercynon-born George Ewart Evans (who was a friend of Morien's father, John).[35] Green wrote to Elaine in October 1962 during the early planning process for the second series of *Dr Finlay's Casebook*: 'we would very much like to have you as a contributor', he explained, before telling her that 'the Finlay series is a winning horse to ride, and worthy of the best jockeys now. The audience re-action has been astonishing.'[36] Almost ten million people tuned in on average to watch.[37]

A couple of months later, at the start of January 1963, with planning now well advanced, Green wrote back hoping that Elaine would write the lead-in episode of the second series.[38] In the event, Elaine's first contribution to *Dr Finlay's Casebook*, 'The Face Saver' was broadcast as the tenth episode of the second series on 8 November 1963, with a repeat on 22 November. The eventual lead-in episode, 'A Time For Laughing', was instead penned by Anthony Coburn, with the series launched on 5 September 1963. Sadly, much of the second series of *Dr Finlay's Casebook* is now lost, including Elaine's episode, with only audience reactions and newspaper criticism left to give a sense of how it was received. Writing in *The Stage*, Marjorie Norris lamented the 'almost over-simplified version of the basic Finlay v. Cameron set-up' and concluded that overall it was 'not a story to get excited over even on an ordinary Friday'.[39] The plot centred around the cause of a disfiguring rash, a 'wishy-washy' theme as the Belfast *Telegraph* complained.[40] In Elaine's defence, 'The Face Saver' was written at speed, largely as a favour to Harry Green, and had been fitted into a schedule which included a four-part adaptation of Eric Ambler's *Epitaph for a Spy*, an episode of the Sid James comedy series *Taxi!* and three episodes of *Maigret*.

The latter, which was already well-established as a series before Elaine joined as a scriptwriter, involved the not inconsiderable task of translating for television at least one of Georges Simenon's original novels not then available in English: *La Maison du Juge* published in France in 1940 but in Britain as *Maigret in Exile* only in 1978. A second story, *Maigret Afraid*, was of more recent vintage having been published in Britain in 1961. Fortunately, Elaine recalled later, 'French was Morien's speciality and that helped'. But there was an onus on getting *Maigret* right, not least because television audiences for the series were substantial – more than fourteen million viewers, on average, watched the third run (Elaine's episodes were in the fourth) – and because the approach taken to adaptation had been a faithful one from the beginning.[41] With the exception of a handful of characters, notably Janvier, one of Maigret's team of four, storylines, plots, and company were all true to the source material. The series star, Rupert Davies, had even flown to Simenon's home in Lausanne, Switzerland, to discuss how to approach acting the character of Inspector Maigret.[42] Simenon went on to tell journalists that 'I am very satisfied with the choice of Rupert Davies as Inspector Maigret. I have shown him all Maigret's mannerisms and habits.'[43]

As the scriptwriter, these considerations were largely external to Elaine's work, although the strive for faithfulness meant that she could not, as she had done with *Epitaph for a Spy*, manipulate the dialogue too freely. Perhaps it was for reason of artistic licence that adaptations of classic literature were found to be easier to write and more creative as an endeavour. Elaine's break into this field came as a result of an offer made by Donald Wilson in the spring of 1963. At the time he was planning serials to accompany the launch of BBC Two the following year. Wilson initially invited Elaine to adapt Gustave Flaubert's *Madame Bovary*, although it proved not to be to her taste. 'I'm sorry', she wrote, 'but I'd hate to do this one. Everyone says I'm crazy to pass up the chance of it, and I'm sincerely grateful to you for offering it to me. I'm sure it will be a hit, too. But it's not for me. I don't like any of the people – nor dislike any of them enough to get a kick out of it that way'.[44] Instead she suggested something by Evelyn Waugh or D.H. Lawrence, or even short series of the Father Brown stories by G.K. Chesterton.

Madame Bovary, in the end, was adapted for television by Giles Cooper (1918-1966), the lead writer on *Maigret*, whereas Elaine's first classic serial for the new channel was Elizabeth Gaskell's novel, *Mary Barton*. Broadcast in the summer of 1964, it received enthusiastic reviews. *The Stage*, for example, thought it 'enthralling television'.[45] *Mary Barton* had, in fact, not been Elaine's original choice to adapt – she preferred the 1931 novel *Juan in America* by the Penarth-born Erik Linklater. With its American dialogue and prohibition-era capers, Elaine felt it would be a natural fit for television, but it has never made it onto the small screen. Ultimately, Wilson felt, *Mary Barton* fitted better into a sequence of classic drama serials which included *Madame Bovary* and the feminist novel, *Ann Veronica,* by H.G. Wells. Wilson added his own adaptation of John Buchan's 1927 novel, *Witch Wood*, with its themes of religious conflict and superstition in the Scottish Lowlands – it was to be his last serial as a BBC employee, on his retirement he began working on his most famous work: John Galsworthy's *The Forsyte Saga*. It aired to great acclaim in 1967.

Following Donald Wilson's departure from the BBC, Elaine became much bolder in her own dealings with the corporation and less deferent to those with whom she spoke, although not always with the level of success she had enjoyed with Donald Wilson. In May 1966, she wrote directly to Sydney Newman to introduce herself as 'one of your more versatile, professional, and highly paid script writers' and to propose a series based on Eric Berne's remarkable 1964 bestseller, *Games People Play*.[46] Elaine continued:

> I've been in this game over ten years and I am certain this would be new, different, up-to-date, and very powerful. Somebody will do it soon anyway because it's a natural.

The series was tentatively called *The Third Degree* and to consider love and sex, success and failure, money, ambition, crime, and the layers of human relationships in between. It would, Elaine thought, 'go like a bomb in America. This book is their new Bible'. Newman thought it interesting, but the idea fell by the wayside nonetheless. As did Elaine's proposal for a series called *The Observers*, which had as its theme the study of human habits by a pair of ethnologists. Verity Lambert, in her comments on the outline, thought it 'a very original series idea and it could be a very good one ... it is certainly worth following up'.[47] The men invited to comment, however, despite recognising the novelty of the programme, found reason not to proceed. Anthony Read, at the time script editor for *The Troubleshooters* and a former scriptwriter for *Z Cars*, thought the idea 'immoral' at its core boiling down to 'a couple of people interfering with the lives of others for no other reason than their own satisfaction'. I think, Read concluded bitingly, 'she should be persuaded to pour her energy into a one-off play on this subject and leave us to pour ours into something that is more worthwhile as series entertainment'.[48]

The second half of the 1960s, with comments like these, which Elaine would not in any case have seen, were an understandably fallow period relative to other times in her career. Between the conclusion of *Lil* in the spring of 1966, which was written for and commissioned by BBC Wales, in any case, and the transmission of *The Doctors* (a medical drama to which Elaine was a contributing writer) in November 1969, her work for national BBC television was largely confined to *Dr Finlay's Casebook*, although she also wrote for *The Onedin Line* and for *King of the River*. Unsurprisingly, she wrote more for ITV – six scripts between 1967 and 1975 – than at any other time, and was a much more regular contributor to regional television in Wales.[49] There was no notion that she wished to defect to commercial television, retaining her life-long allegiance to the BBC, but frustration with regular rejections at a national level was apparent. For a while, London producers kept Elaine in the mix, inviting her to provide pilot scripts to proposed vehicles for Thora Hird, on the one hand, and Virginia McKenna, on the other. The Hird series was eventually made using a script and concept by Philip Levene: *The First Lady*. Elaine had proposed a storyline focusing on the eviction of a family and the intervention of Hird's character, whereas the successful script proved to be one about a down-to-earth woman councillor dealing with problems within local government.[50]

Having lost out on *The First Lady*, Elaine was able to undertake a commission from BBC Wales: *One of the Family*, a fifteen-part series starring, amongst others, Margaret John and Windsor Davies. Like *Lil* a few years earlier, the series was intended to provide true-to-life characters in readily identifiable locations and circumstances. The opening scene was a quasi-Iain Banks-esque turn involving a funeral and a family gathering. Davies played Trefor Roberts, an unmarried electrician who is foreman at the local factory. The rest of the Roberts family of the fictional 'Abereithin' in the South Wales Valleys included Olwen who had 'married out of her class' to a company director, Mansel, and the youngest daughter, Kay, who found the family too stifling and had fled to London.[51] With the first series having proved itself popular with viewers, a second series was commissioned for broadcast in the autumn of 1969, whereas in the first Elaine had equally shared writing with one of the cast, David Garfield, for the second Garfield took on the majority of the work. The temper of some of the characters was thus altered, leading to a mellower and less class-aware narrative. The tempestuous relationship between Olwen and Mansel, which had been an important part of the first series turned into a situation wherein they accepted 'rather than aggravate[d] a far from perfect union'.[52]

Of her three Welsh serials, only *One of the Family* failed to make it to the national television network. Set alongside *A Matter of Degree* and *Lil*, however, it served as a clear illustration of Elaine's views about post-war South Wales and the changes in society that had taken place therein. The characters were factory workers, not miners; women were presented as more rebellious and endowed with greater freedom, rather than as the 'Welsh mam' of more traditional literary portraits, and communities seemed to thrive as much on gossip as they did trade union politics. However, in the 1970s, Elaine turned away from her own creations towards adaptations of major literary works and biographical one offs or serials. These recovered her status as a leading scriptwriter, which had faded somewhat in the late-1960s when producers' tastes did not tally with Elaine's creative output and her range of ideas. Adaptation meant sacrificing originality, somewhat, in favour of saleability. This made her different from her contemporaries, such as Gwyn Thomas and Alun Richards, who were more original in their output; although they were short story writers and novelists, as well as playwrights and screenwriters, which undoubtedly shaped their approach to television and radio, and provided material of their own to adapt.

All of those involved in adapting work for television or radio (or, indeed, the cinema) face inevitable choices about character, plot, scene, and setting. In recent times, Andrew Davies has described his own approach: adding in the male perspective when adapting Jane Austen, for example, or sexualising Tolstoy's *War and Peace* in ways out of keeping with the source material but necessary for televisual excitement, or not being afraid to add in scenes where necessary.[53] Elaine faced the same dilemmas: how far can the scriptwriter innovate, change, or improve, without the audience feeling that the source material had been abandoned? How original dare be the adaptor? In some cases, particularly in her reworking of *How Green Was My Valley*, Elaine changed the story substantially, adding in far greater authenticity than was apparent in the source material; in others she retained the spirit of the original work conscious of her own admiration for the authors or the characters. But when Elaine set out to adapt, in succession, *A Pin to see the Peepshow*, *Anne of Avonlea*, and *How Green Was My Valley*, there were relatively few models on which should could base her approach to this kind of writing – Donald Wilson's *The Forsyte Saga* having the greatest impact of all. Elaine had to come up with rules of her own, answer her own questions about innovation and invention, and settle in her own mind the balance between faithfulness and televisual efficacy. The result was some of the most famous and enduring television adaptations of the late twentieth century. Most of her work has never been bettered and has never been remade.

FIVE
TESTAMENTS OF YOUTH

In the summer of 1973, Elaine returned to national television with her first major serial for BBC Two for almost a decade. She had been asked to adapt Fryniwyd Tennyson Jesse's 1934 novel *A Pin to see the Peepshow*. Based on the famous and controversial trial of Edith Thompson and Freddy Bywaters in 1922, the novel provided a thinly fictionalised account of the case and the grip of convention and norms of respectability on women of the period. Elaine explained her approach to the novel, and her own reaction to it, in her introduction for the Virago edition published in 1979. She wrote,

> When I was asked to adapt the book for television I got hold of a transcript of the Thompson and Bywaters trial and made enquiries about Edith Thompson, thinking that conceivably the author of the novel had garnished Julia with a spurious vulnerability and charm to gain our sympathy, and distorted the judicial proceedings to strengthen her case. I learned that most of the people who had known Edith Thompson – women as well as men – were hot in her defence, and that the facts which emerged in the trial, except for the substitution of a spanner for a knife, were as described.[1]

As she read through the novel, Elaine regarded it – as many readers have done – as an English version of Gustave Flaubert's nineteenth-century French classic, *Madame Bovary*, whose adaptation she had once refused, until she reached the final passages involving the retelling of the Thompson and Bywaters trial. Then the character of Julia Almond, played in the series by Francesca Annis (alongside Bernard Hepton as Herbert Starling), emerged as something otherwise – as a woman trapped by 'the aura of sexual prejudice (as palpable as anti-semitism, apartheid or any other form of paranoia) which pervaded the court where she was tried'. What made the revival of *A Pin to see the Peepshow* relevant as well as dramatically interesting was the contemporary debate surrounding the death penalty, which had been abolished on mainland Britain (for most crimes except treason) in 1965 and in Northern Ireland in 1973. As Elaine concluded,

> You cannot reverse a hanging. So the book's final anger is directed against the whole apparatus of judicial execution. The last chapters should be compulsory reading for anyone who still believes, for whatever high-minded reasons, that the death penalty ought to be re-introduced.

A Pin to see the Peepshow proved enormously popular and a critical success; Elaine won the first of a series of writing awards given for her television work: the 1973 Screen Writer's Guild prize for best dramatization.[2] This marked the beginning of a string of nearly a dozen high-profile and highly-successful adaptations of literary works and biographies which lasted until Elaine's retirement from scriptwriting at the end of the 1980s. This was the period in which Elaine won her BAFTAs, further Screen Writer's Guild awards, Royal Television Society awards for writer of the year and outstanding contribution to regional television, and the Prix Italia. Critics, including the Australian poet and memoirist, Clive James, praised 'a writer who combines sensitivity with analytical power'.[3] That was in 1977, a few years later he added to his view:

Elaine Morgan's adaptations are miles more interesting than almost anything produced by the name playwrights, whose alleged originality is so often the merest clamour.[4]

Actors were now keen to be part of productions which Elaine had written: as Sian Phillips recalled, 'if you saw that name on a script then you really wanted to do it'.[5] For directors as well as television viewers and prize panels, it was difficult to disagree that Elaine Morgan had entered her golden age of screenwriting.

Whereas *A Pin to see the Peepshow* heralded Elaine's turn to adapting literary works for television, it was her subsequent *Horizon* documentary, 'Joey', which most obviously signalled her emergence as a mature writer for television. In the summer of 1974, she was sent a copy of Joey Deacon's ground-breaking autobiography *Tongue Tied* with a view to scripting a television adaptation.[6] Deacon, who became a well-known celebrity because of the book, suffered from severe cerebral palsy and had been in hospital almost his entire life. He dictated the book to friends (who were amongst the few people able to understand him) over a period of more than fourteen months. Some of Deacon's story had first been aired in a radio documentary broadcast in 1971 but the appearance of his autobiography enabled a more thorough depiction of his life. Elaine co-wrote the script with the programme's director, Brian Gibson (1944-2004). 'Joey' aired on BBC Two on 9 December 1974. It was typically hard-hitting, with one reviewer noting that 'perhaps the greatest compliment that can be paid to this first-rate reconstruction of Joey Deacon's autobiography *Tongue Tied*, is that it left one feeling humble at such an incredible victory of the human spirit'.[7] It was a major award-winner, including the BAFTA for 'best specialised television programme' and the Prix Italia for television documentary.[8] Two years after its original broadcast, 'Joey' was chosen as the 1974 entry in a special series of programmes to mark twenty-five years of BBC TV, highlighting both the programme's significance and Elaine's cachet.[9]

Three works from the 1970s served as Elaine's signature pieces: *How Green Was My Valley* from 1975-76; the five-part series based on the life of Marie Curie broadcast in 1977; and her 1979 adaptation of Vera Brittain's First World War memoir, *Testament of Youth*. The latter led to a resurgence in the book's popularity, which had faded significantly by the time of Brittain's death in 1970, and it has subsequently never been out of print. Reissued by Virago in its modern classics series in April 1978, *Testament of Youth* revitalised public interest in the role of women during the First World War introducing new generations to the social history of the period. There were soon calls for it to be made into a television series.[10] The key figure at the BBC was script editor Betty Willingale, who had previously worked on *I, Claudius* (1976) and *Tinker, Tailor, Soldier, Spy* (1979). It was Willingale who contacted Elaine – 'I was the 1970s equivalent of Andrew Davies' Elaine recalled, 'a safe pair of hands, with 26 years' experience of writing for television under my belt' – as the first-choice to pen the adaptation. Although familiar with *Testament of Youth* in outline, Elaine had yet to read it – she quickly identified with Brittain and the parallel lives they led at Oxford. As Elaine wrote many years later in the *Western Mail*,

> I was also a great admirer of Vera Brittain and had several things in common with her. She went up to Oxford from the provinces when very few females did that – so did I. She was there in the First World War: I was there in the second. A young man who wrote poems to and about her was killed in the war – and the same thing happened to me.

Although she stuck carefully to the source material, conscious that Brittain's daughter, the then cabinet minister Shirley Williams, was keen to ensure that the adaptation was as accurate as possible, this later memory shows that Elaine was all-too aware of her own past. Indeed, the publication in 1978 of Michael Sharp's edited collection of Drummond Allison's poetry, which for the first time included all of the poems written by Allison to Elaine, brought 'the same thing' very much into focus once more. As she wrote about Roland Leighton, Elaine undoubtedly mused privately about Allison. Elaine met Shirley Williams during the initial read through of episode one of *Testament of Youth*. She described the encounter in the *Western Mail* in 2010, following the release of the DVD of the series:

> I was very nervous when Shirley was invited ... But her only comment concerned a scene depicting Vera on a tennis court, exchanging remarks with her partner while preparing to serve. Shirley said that on the tennis court Vera was totally focused and would never have engaged in casual banter. I later heard that having seen the finished product there was one thing Shirley regretted. Her father made his entrance in the final episode, and she felt he was appreciably more handsome than the actor chosen to play him.[11]

Writing in the *Observer*, Clive James noted that the series 'was one of the best things I have seen on television' since the BBC's adaptation of Muriel Spark's 1963 novel *The Girls of Slender Means* in 1975. He again praised 'Elaine Morgan's literate adaption', in which the 'two lines of narrative form a powerful sad counterpoint' and wondered (with tongue in cheek) whether 'the BBC is engaged in a vast conspiracy to make Shirley Williams Prime Minister'.[12] The series was widely feted: Cheryl Campbell won both the BAFTA and Broadcasting Press Guild awards for her portrayal of Vera Brittain; the series won the BAFTA for Best Drama, too. Elaine was herself declared writer of the year by the Royal Television Society in 1980.[13]

Marie Curie, which starred Jane Lapotaire and Nigel Hawthorne as Marie and her husband Pierre, was an adaptation of Robert Reid's 1974 biography and produced by the BBC and Time-Life for broadcast on both sides of the Atlantic.[14] To underscore authenticity, particularly in the field of science, it was overseen by Peter Goodchild – previously the editor of *Horizon*, and from 1980-1984 the BBC's head of science programming.[15] The aim of Reid's biography, and the subsequent television series, was to present a more truthful version of Marie Curie's life than could be found in the 1943 Hollywood biopic, *Madame Curie*.[16] As one television reviewer put it, 'what emerges is a woman who is much less romantic but no less heroic'.[17] Another observed that, rather than present a romantic vision 'if anything Elaine Morgan's script was likely to err ... towards a tub thumping women's lib approach'.[18] That was not, of course, the point – Elaine's version of Marie Curie was conscious of her towering scientific achievements, her political commitments, and of the personal sacrifices made in the discovery of both radium and polonium, and her theory of radioactivity. The series, which was quickly identified as a probable award-winner by critics, won the 1977 BAFTA for best drama series, beating *When The Boat Comes In, The Norman Conquests*, and the Granada adaptation of Charles Dickens's *Hard Times*.[19]

Whereas *Testament of Youth* and *Marie Curie* provided Elaine with the chance to produce faithful adaptations of the source material, albeit with a knowing eye to similar experiences in the case of the former, her work on Richard Llewellyn's *How Green Was My Valley* saw her alter, radically, both the intent and the pulse of the original novel. Perhaps the most enduring of Elaine's Welsh adaptations, the 1975-76 series encapsulated her attempt to bridge the gap between fictional representations of the South Wales Coalfield and its past, her absorption and family connections to that history, and a desire to convey the reasons for the radical politics of her family, of her community, and of her own. Indeed, she rejected Llewellyn's deeply conservative mythology and setting, reworking the novel's politics by drawing on the experiences and writings of her father-in-law, John E. Morgan, and his friend Morgan Walters. Gilfach Goch, the setting of the novel, was largely exchanged for Ynysybwl where Morien had grown up; and Llewellyn's errors of fact and detail were exchanged the reality drawn directly from John E. Morgan's diaries, which Morien had been transcribing from the original shorthand. Even Morien's own sickly childhood, which saw him bed bound in a similar manner to Huw Morgan, the novel's protagonist, was adapted to add to the drama and to the veracity of the narrative.

Honesty was conveyed by the largely Welsh cast, too, with Stanley Baker and Sian Phillips in the leading roles, as well as in the choice of shooting locations.[20] In keeping with this attempt to make an authentic programme, *How Green Was My Valley* was filmed in and around the South Wales Valleys, as would have been expected, at various locations such as, for the first and second episodes, for example, Tirpentwys Colliery near Crumlin, Tabor Baptist Chapel at Cwmafan near Port Talbot, Tyderwen primary school in Nantyffyllon, and in Dynevor Street in Fochriw, near Rhymney. The latter has since been demolished and so the series provides a record of the housing stock there towards the very end of their life. But filming, importantly, did not take place in Gilfach Goch – the community Llewellyn had intended for his novel. With all her amendments to character and setting, politics and ethos,

Elaine enabled easy rejection of the Llewellyn mythology. She was subtle enough, though, by this stage in her career, to make alterations so as to not misdirect those who had read the novel or seen the earlier Hollywood film and were familiar with its points of view; instead she took familiarity and made it true to life.

Such significant changes were made possible by the fact that, as one reviewer noted, the novel 'has long held the familiar position of the work that everyone has heard of but fewer and fewer actually have read'.[21] The catalyst for the adaptation, the first since 1960, was the publication of Richard Llewellyn's belated, Welsh Arts Council-funded sequel *Green, Green My Valley Now* which was published early in 1975 and saw Huw Morgan return to his native South Wales after a successful career abroad in Patagonia to discover what had happened in the years since his departure. Earlier sequels to *How Green Was My Valley* had explored Huw's life in Patagonia, and those works are alluded to in one of the maps which adorned the inside covers of the first edition of *Green, Green My Valley Now*.[22] As Dai Smith has noted, the other map included on the cover is of a Wales which is 'bottomless ... starts around Builth Wells, extends north to the Lleyn peninsula and omits all of industrial South Wales'. But why the absence? As Smith rightly argues, the 'proletarian universality' of *that* South Wales – of Labour Country, as I have referred to it elsewhere, – 'can have no place in a timeless Welsh world'.[23] A world in which subjugation came not from the coalowners or the ironmasters, but from the external other: in Llewellyn's words, 'Romans, Saxons, and the brothers of the Norman bastard and their sons, and on, until, with time, they called themselves English'.

The politics of Llewellyn's original version of *How Green Was My Valley* were, if anything, worse than those evident in its later sequels. In his study of the novel, the literary critic Aidan Byrne has suggested that 'How Green Was My Valley espouse[d] a populist neo-fascist modernism founded in rejecting industrialism, sexual freedom, democracy and ultimately rationalism both ideologically and narratively'.[24] Elaine, of course, did not share Llewellyn's perspective or his politics and created a version which had far more sympathy for the socialist communitarianism which the novel had derided. She condensed and invented characters particularly in the Morgan family, renamed others, and weeded the plot. Some of the reworkings were slight – Huw Morgan's love interest, for example, known as Ceinwen Phillips in the novel is called Ceinwen Lloyd in the series. Other changes were more substantial. The Morgan family, which consisted of thirteen members in the novel, was shrunk in size – Gwilym Jr and was excised entirely and the characters of Ianto and Davy merged together. To preserve the character of Marged, her relationship with Gwilym Jr was transferred to the amalgam, too. Elaine's version of Ianto, as portrayed by Keith Drinkel in the series, was close in temperament and narrative to the Davy of the novel but distinctive enough to be a clear invention. Certainly, the trade union politics of Ianto in 1975 were much sharper and more authentic than those of Davy in 1939.

Indeed, Ianto, as Elaine imagined him, bore more than a passing resemblance to her father-in-law, John E. Morgan of Ynysybwl. He had been a trade union firebrand in his youth and a pioneer of the Social Democratic Federation, the Independent Labour Party, and the South Wales Miners' Federation. For a period in the 1940s, he was also a member of the Communist Party. Serving as secretary of the Lady Windsor Lodge for most of the first half of the twentieth century, he was perhaps the longest-serving trade union official in the Federation's history and was an active proselytiser for the Miners' Next Step in 1912. He certainly had read works by Friedrich Engels and the Scottish philosopher Winwood Reade –

not least Reade's secularist classic, *The Martyrdom of Man* (1872) – books which Ianto discovered on Rev. Gruffydd's shelf and, as a result, came to the realisation that the minister was as radical as himself. The two then bonded over their mutual enthusiasm for the politics of Keir Hardie. Owen, the most practical of the Morgan brothers, who was often shown to be tinkering in his shed, was similarly modelled on a real family member – in this case, Elaine's father, Billy Floyd. He, too, had been an inventor and enjoyed tinkering with materials – fixing and inventing as he went along.

Elaine radically altered the implications of *How Green Was My Valley* and its reading of the South Walian past, restoring (as much as possible) the realities of class politics and gender relations, and evacuating Llewellyn's own 'obsessive border separation between individuals, classes and ethnic groups'.[25] Indeed, any sense of Gwilym Morgan senior's racist hostility to outsiders, particularly to the writers and philosophers that Ianto and Davy had read (such as the German Karl Marx or the Englishman H.M. Hyndman), which form a clear part of the familial disagreements over trade union activity in the novel, disappeared from the television script. Ironically, given the excision of Llewellyn's expressions of racial sentiment, the BBC got into trouble in 1977 when it emerged that the series had been shown in apartheid South Africa, despite a ban on programmes featuring Equity members being sold to the country.[26] The reworking of Llewellyn's characters and aspects of the storyline made the television series far more compelling than the novel, although some contemporary reviewers nevertheless regarded the adaptation as riddled with cliche and, in the case of the *Daily Mirror*'s critic, Clifford Davis, easily dismissed as 'very Welsh, very sentimental, very dated'.[27]

By her own admission, supported by a scribbled note on the commissioning documentation held at the BBC archives, Elaine was not the BBC's first choice to adapt *How Green Was My Valley* for television. Indeed, her involvement in the production seems to have been an accident. The role of scriptwriter had originally been intended for Emlyn Williams. As a playwright for theatre, Williams was enormously successful, but he had relatively little experience of television and eventually turned down the commission. Elaine recalled the moment she was brought in: 'for whatever reason, they found themselves with the dates pencilled in ... rehearsal date looming uncomfortably close, and no scripts that everyone was entirely happy with. They turned to the old hoss'. To produce the six fifty-minute episodes, which were written at high speed, Elaine worked closely with script editor Betty Willingale, with whom she developed a strong and successful partnership in the years afterwards, and the series producer Martin Lisemore. When Lisemore died suddenly two years later aged thirty-seven in a car crash, Elaine was one of a group of writers, producers and actors who staged a special memorial show in London – Elaine helped to pen the script alongside the creator of *Crossroads* Peter Ling, *Avengers* and *The Sweeney* writer Richard Harris, and Neville Phillips whose credits included *The Dick Emery Show*.[28]

Elaine's role in adapting *How Green Was My Valley* was first announced in late August 1975, the scripts having been delivered by the end of July, a few months after the publication of Llewellyn's sequel and a few months prior to the broadcast of the first episode on 29 December.[29] The series was one of a number of adaptations of Welsh literary works that year, many of them scripted by Elaine: in the summer, BBC Radio 4 broadcast her four-part adaptation of Alexander Cordell's bestseller, *Rape of the Fair Country* (1959), which detailed the emerging class conflict and the early chartist movement in Blaenafon, one of the more prominent iron towns of early nineteenth century South Wales. Cordell's own left-wing politics were readily evident both in the novel and in the radio play, and Elaine had little difficulty in matching Cordell's ideas about the region with her own. By coincidence, Stanley Baker, who was to take the lead role of Gwilym Morgan in Elaine's adaptation of *How Green Was My Valley*, had himself sought to develop a big screen adaptation of Cordell's novel a few years earlier, but failed in his attempt to do so. 'There's not enough bread around', he lamented to journalists in 1971.[30]

The significance of Elaine's 'Welsh turn' in the 1970s and 1980s, which also included the *Life and Times of David Lloyd George* in 1981 and the 1978 adaptation of Jack Jones's fictionalised account of composer Joseph Parry's life in the United States, *Off to Philadelphia in the Morning*, lay in the presentation of Welsh history to audiences who were not otherwise widely exposed to it. In this regard, Elaine become one of the leading popular exponents of ideas about Wales and its past at a time when a new generation of historians, and labour history societies such as Llafur, were reshaping critical understanding of similar moments. The two strands did not always meet in the middle, particularly on questions of gender, but Elaine's personal sympathies were broadly similar to those of the historians and were focused on the people of the valleys and their proletarian universality.[31] Her miners and their wives may not have been 'voters in the terraces', as Gwyn Thomas depicted them, but neither were they the thin caricatures of conservative and nationalist mythology. By placing Wales and its history on television, Elaine was undoubtedly adding to contemporary conversation about self-government: she was an active supporter of devolution, both in the 1979 referendum campaign and again in 1997. Speaking at a meeting of writers in Cardiff during the latter campaign, for instance, she insisted that 'those opposed to devolution suffer from a terminal lack of self-esteem and self-confidence'.[32]

Holding up the mirror and presenting the history of Wales on television and radio was precisely about projecting esteem, confidence and self-awareness, which Elaine achieved whilst not resting too heavily on what was otherwise a largely male-orientated historical record. Indeed, although historians such as Deirdre Beddoe, Angela John and Ursula Masson deserve credit for their recovery of Welsh women's history, Elaine's own contribution to popular understanding was itself significant. This sensitivity to women's history was very much on display in one Elaine's rare offerings for ITV: an adaptation of George Ewart Evans's short story 'Possessions', which was broadcast in May 1974.[33] Directed by John Irvin, who later made his name as the director of the BBC's acclaimed adaptation of John Le Carré's *Tinker, Tailor, Soldier, Spy* (1979), and starring Anthony Hopkins (as the ragman, Dando Hamer), the programme focused on a hard-up Welsh mother who refused to sell her belongings to survive the interwar Depression. *Possessions* was the final part of a series of television plays about childhood written or adapted by, amongst others, Keith Waterhouse and actor Barbara Waring. Although reviewers felt that the the artificial nature of the series made it more difficult for viewers to perceive the common threads of discussion, they nevertheless felt that *Possessions* was 'credible, lovable and gently amusing'.

With hindsight, the appeal of George Ewart Evans's short story to Elaine is not difficult to understand. The loss of a father at a young age; the collapse of the family business and the impact of the Depression; the struggle of a mother to survive against the odds; these were all themes very close to Elaine's own experiences or those of her family. The story began:

A month after my father died they sold up the shop to pay the debts. Our big family and the pit-strikes had knocked the stuffing

out of the grocery business and after my father's death it passed
out without a whimper. The only bit of stock left after the sell-up
was the pony and cart. My mother had held on to the pony by
swearing it was hers – down in the books in her name; but even
then, if she hadn't been pretty downright with the auctioneer, a
big chap with smooth skin and an expensive, whisky complexion,
they'd have put the pony under the hammer as well. They left the
cart because it wasn't worth taking away. Ma hung on to the old
piano with the pleated silk front. The auctioneer had walked
around it, mumbled that it would fetch a pound or two and ought
by rights to be sold up with the other things, but Ma had stood
her ground over this, too.

But this was not simply an admiring writer adapting another's work
from afar. George Ewart Evans was well-known to Morien's family
in Ynysybwl, particularly to his father John E. Morgan with whom
Evans maintained a long-standing friendship.[34] Evans had been born
in the nearby village of Abercynon and grown up into the left-wing
political circles which contained, amongst others, Emrys Hughes
the Labour MP for South Ayrshire between 1946 and 1970.[35] *Possessions* was a signal of Elaine's mature and confident ability to adapt
Welsh material for wide audiences by the mid-1970s. She had
served her apprenticeship as an adapter of literary works a decade
earlier, when writing the four-part adaptation of Elizabeth Gaskell's
novel *Mary Barton* for BBC Scotland. It was broadcast on BBC
Two in 1964. Although distinct in accent and chronology from the
later Welsh adaptations, Gaskell's novel provided an opportunity to
develop working-class characters involved in trade union activity
and industrial disputes – an obvious crossover with her subsequent
version of *How Green Was My Valley*.[36]

The latter work also had several influences on Elaine's master-
piece for television, *The Life and Times of David Lloyd George*,

which starred Philip Madoc in the title role and was broadcast to critical acclaim in 1981.[37] The opening scenes were similarly located in a Welsh wilderness accompanied by stirring title music – in the case of *Life and Times*, the haunting 'Chi Mai' by the giant of contemporary film composition, Ennio Morricone. Viewed retrospectively, the poignant penultimate episode of the series, 'Win or Lose', broadcast in April 1981, spoke both to the past and to the present; the splits in personality and politics which dogged the Liberal Party after the First World War seemed to echo those which were contemporaneously wreaking havoc in the Labour Party. Four months earlier, the Gang of Four, including Vera Brittain's daughter Shirley Williams, had signalled their growing discontent with the Labour Party in the Limehouse Declaration. 'Won't it cause a lot of bitterness if you have Liberals standing against each other?', asks one character pointedly. 'Now let's make one thing clear', Lloyd George reacts sharply, Philip Madoc's deep voice conveying both anger and hurt simultaneously, 'I'm not the one who wants a split'.

Labour Party politics was even more overtly examined in her version of Howard Spring's 1940 novel, *Fame is the Spur*, which was broadcast in 1982. Starring Tim Piggott-Smith as John 'Hamer' Shawcross, who was widely regarded as having been based on Ramsay MacDonald, Labour's first Prime Minister who eventually split the party in 1931, the series chimed with contemporary debates about the direction and purpose of the Labour Party, particularly in the aftermath of the Social Democratic Party's formation the previous year. We might speculate in retrospect which of the leading figures from Labour's recent past Elaine had in mind when writing the scripts for this series – it was not the only occasion in the early 1980s when Labour's internecine conflicts found their way into her work, whether by coincidence or design.[38] Certainly, the themes of Spring's novel, which showed both working-class firebrands becoming steadily absorbed into the upper-class environment which they had once denounced, and their erstwhile comrades who remained loyal to the cause, were of contemporary relevance. Nor was this adaptation out of keeping with Elaine's 'Welsh turn'. Several sections of the novel, and thus the television series, were set in Spring's native South Wales. In episode five, Shawcross was shown in the Rhondda during the industrial upheavals of 1910-1912.[39] With a cameo by Keir Hardie, the mining sections of the series provided a quasi-sequel to her version of *How Green Was My Valley*.

By the mid-1980s, Elaine began to write less for television focusing primarily on one off biographical programmes such as those about artists Gwen John and Stanley Spencer, the scientists Alfred Wallace and Gregor Mendel, the playwright George Bernard Shaw, and the Egyptologist Amelia B. Edwards.[40] Two works from this final period of scriptwriting stand out, neveretheless, as a continuation of both her interests in women's history and the history of the labour movement. *The Burston Rebellion* from 1985, which was nominated for a Broadcasting Press Guild prize, and the four part adaptation of *The Diary of Anne Frank* which aired in 1987 to coincide with the fortieth anniversary of the book's first publication in Dutch.[41] *The Burston Rebellion* was a dramatization of the school strike which began in the Norfolk village of Burston in 1914 and did not end until 1939. The series starred Eileen Atkins and Bernard Hill and was Elaine's only foray into the history of the county in which she had first taught for the WEA. It seems likely that she first encountered the history of the strike in the 1940s, given that Burston was only a few miles from Diss where Elaine was living. The strike was itself brought back into wider consciousness by Bertram Edwards with his historical account *The Burston School Strike* published by Lawrence and Wishart in 1974. His book provided much of the source material for the series, together with additional research conducted by Betka Zamoyska who wrote the book to accompany the series.[42]

Two school teachers were at the centre of the Burston story: Tom and Annie Higdon.[43] Tom Higdon was from Somerset and Annie from Wallasey near Liverpool; they met whilst teaching in London and first arrived in Norfolk in 1902 to take up a post in a rural school outside Norwich. As socialists and active trade unionists, they were not the typical rural teacher, expected to be subservient to the local education committee and the governing body. Forced out of Wood Dalling in 1911 after a series of conflicts with the education committee, they moved to Burston. They were soon confronted by the local vicar who expected obeisance. They refused. The vicar concocted a 'scandal' whereby Annie Higdon was accused of having caned two orphans in the care of Barnardo's. Although an inquiry found no evidence, both Tom and Annie Higdon were dismissed. This resulted in a school strike led, initially, by a small number of children before expanding considerably – the children were taught in the open air by the Higdons as an alternative to the council school. With backing from the National Union of Teachers, the Higdons added to the traditional curriculum a range of subjects including trade unionism, Christian socialism, and the strike school became a 'centre of rural democracy' surviving until Tom Higdon's death in 1939. Annie Higdon died in 1946.

The themes of *The Burston Rebellion* were thus typical of Elaine's work: socialist activity, the role of women, education, and community responses to victimisation and the malicious effects of capitalism. Produced by Ruth Caleb, who in the 1990s was the first woman appointed as head of drama at BBC Wales (the first anywhere at the BBC), and directed by Norman Stone, *The Burston Rebellion* proved to be a major production which, as one reviewer put it, 'could hardly have gone wrong', and won a series of awards at film and television festivals including a critics award in France, and the Samuel G. Engel award in the United States.[44] Yet it was to be overshadowed by *The Diary of Anne Frank*, which had a much lower profile cast but which nevertheless enjoyed a much higher profile given both the anniversary of the source material and the continued resonance of the Holocaust. In the United States it was nominated for a CableACE award – the cable network equivalent of the Emmy's. Elaine's adaptation was by no means the first for British audiences – there had been a theatre production in the 1950s, for instance, and a radio adaptation by Nigel Lambert in the 1970s – however, it was the first version for television.

The Diary of Anne Frank was broadcast on Sunday afternoons just after five o'clock and was targeted at older children – those who might well have been introduced to the book in school. In the role of Otto Frank was Emrys James, the Welsh actor who had previously starred in *Testament of Youth* as Vera Brittain's father. The problem for at least one reviewer was that the production included not only Emrys James but a range of other English and Welsh actors, including the lead Katharine Schlesinger, whose accents were hardly authentic. 'They live in Amsterdam, which has lots of barges and is also entirely populated by English or Welsh actors ... all very sad'.[45] It does indeed jar to contemporary sensi-bilities, which have now been trained to expect a more truthful soundscape. Nevertheless, Elaine was faithful to the source material dramatizing where necessary and drawing on Anne Frank's own words to provide narration. The series provided an important visual record of one of the most enduring works of twentieth century. There was a welcome echo for Elaine, too. Anne Frank always addressed her diary as 'Kitty', the imagined personality she invented and to whom she wrote her thoughts. Kitty, of course, had been the name of Elaine's first character, about whom she had written in her short story in the *Cardiff Times* more than fifty years earlier.

The final series with which Elaine was involved as scriptwriter was the BBC's popular adaptation of Margery Allingham's Campion series, starring the former *Doctor Who* and *All Things Great and Small* actor, Peter Davison, in the title role. Alongside Alan Plater (who in the 1990s went on to champion the work of Gwyn Thomas), Jill Hyem, and the scriptwriter of *Upstairs, Downstairs* Jeremy Paul, Elaine was invited to adapt one of the novels for the first series. In her case, *Death of a Ghost* which was first published in 1934. Although the two part series was certainly well-received by audiences, it was by no means a great send-off after almost thirty five years of writing for television and radio, and undoubtedly the most light-weight literary adaptation with which Elaine had been involved for quite some time. Indeed, the muted nature of 'retirement' from screenwriting suggests that it was, perhaps, not entirely anticipated; although as she suggested in her autobiography her ability, aged almost seventy, to concentrate on the process had begun to wane. In the end, Elaine felt herself too old-fashioned:

> It would be nice to claim that I then retired leaving them wanting more – that's what people in showbiz are always urged to do. It wouldn't be true though It was no longer an asset to have been in at the beginning: too many things had changed. Techniques had changed. The audience's expectations had changed, and their attention span shortened. Different people were in charge and used very different criteria for judging a script.

Perhaps as compensation, and in recognition of her status as one of the most senior scriptwriters in the country in the early 1990s, Elaine found herself occasionally employed as a judge in competitions to find the next generation of writing talent.[46] This recalled her involvement in writers' clubs in Aberdare, Abertillery, Cardiff and Neath decades before and her work teaching film and television scriptwriting for the adult and continuing education department at University College Swansea in the 1980s.[47] Elaine's final scripted broadcast, fittingly, was a segment for *Woman's Hour* – 'the anthropologist' – aired on 2 November 1990. It was almost forty years, to the day, since she had first sat in front of a radio microphone.

As if to signal her acceptance of this fate, in 1990 Elaine donated her copies of her scripts to the South Wales Miners' Library, where they joined the library of Gwyn Thomas and Lewis Jones's diaries as part of a growing collection of materials relating to Welsh writers from the South Wales Coalfield.[48] This was followed four years later by the award of a Fellowship by University College Swansea in recognition of Elaine's contribution to Welsh life.[49] Although her work for television and radio had come to an end, her work as a writer was by no means over, and Elaine began her seventies engaged in scientific debates about human evolution. Indeed, it was as an amateur anthropologist that Elaine (re-)gained worldwide recognition in the 1990s, somewhat overshadowing her television career as the number of repeats declined and materials became difficult to access: few of Elaine's serials were released on VHS or DVD and many of her older programmes were wiped in the 1960s. Having turned away from science as a schoolgirl convinced that it would be easier to win a place at Oxford through the Arts, Elaine turned back to her older enthusiasms publishing more frequently in the fields of evolutionary biology and anthropology than ever she had as a dramatist, at least in book form. It all began, of course, with someone else's bestseller: Desmond Morris's 1967 classic, *The Naked Ape.*[50]

SIX
EVOLUTION

One day, not long after *The Naked Ape* had been published and serialised in the *Daily Mirror*, Elaine came home from Mountain Ash library with a copy in her hand to read. As she made her way through the book, and other literature to which it made reference by writers such as Robert Ardrey and Konrad Lorenz, she found herself getting increasingly frustrated. 'The more I read of this genre', she wrote later, 'the more I found that the fascination was being modified, and in the end swamped, by a much stronger emotion': anger. Reflecting on the paradox at the heart of the Tarzanist theory of evolution – namely that if men had lost their body hair running around on the savannah, what explanation was there for women having lost theirs – Elaine soon began to think the idea that men had the sole responsibility for evolution, that women had 'little or no part in the evolutionary stage except to bear the next generation of hunters', was all nonsense. Yet, at the time, Morris's theory, including the idea that humans are apes and beneath the cultural facade of modernity lay instincts and behaviours that could only be explained in terms of evolutionary biology and animal ancestors, was hardly controversial.

For a while, Elaine waited for someone else to have the same reaction she had had and publish a response. None was forthcoming. Realising that she would have to write the book herself, Elaine picked up her pen and began with these words:

> According to the Book of Genesis, God first created man. Woman
> was not only an afterthought, but an amenity. For close on two
> thousand years this holy scripture was believed to justify her sub-
> ordination and explain her inferiority; for even as a copy, she was
> not a very good copy. There were differences. She was not one of
> His best efforts.

They are the opening lines to her 1972 best seller, *The Descent
of Woman*. Polemical and spirited, it dismissed phallocentric theories of evolutionary biology and instead argued for the equal
role of women in the evolution of humans. The book was published at a serendipitous moment and caught the zeitgeist of the
women's liberation movement across Britain and abroad, particularly in the United States. It was quickly, and widely, translated
into a variety of languages and made Elaine, to borrow the words
of historian Deirdre Beddoe, into 'one of the stars of international
feminism'.[1] This all came about, Elaine would always insist, by
chance. If someone else had come along, Elaine would have been
content to be a bystander in the battle against the Tarzanists. But
in another writer's hands, I think, the argument would have been
far less impactful and the book would not still be in print nearly
half a century later.[2] 'I find the whole yarn pretty incredible',
Elaine wrote, setting out her case in the opening pages of *Descent
of Woman*

> Desmond Morris, pondering on the shape of a woman's breasts,
> instantly deduces that they evolved because her mate became a
> Mighty Hunter, and defends this preposterous proposition with
> the greatest ingenuity. There's something about the Tarzan figure
> which has them all mesmerized.[3]

But what has Tarzan got to do with the evolution of Jane, Elaine pondered, there had to be another answer besides women existing for the needs of men.

A passing reference in *The Naked Ape* to the work of an Oxford University biologist, Sir Alister Hardy, on a possible aquatic phase of human evolution provided the basis of Elaine's alternative theory that 'woman evolved in her own interest'. She began writing in October 1969, corresponding with Hardy, seeking his advice on and, more surreptitiously, his blessing for, a 'popular book on the subject' of the aquatic ape.[4] Hardy was a little nervous at first, protective of his own research, but soon relented hoping that new work would engender a resurgence of interest in the theory. When *Descent of Woman* was completed, a year or so later, Elaine sent it on to Harvey Unna who replied within a few days, full of praise and convinced of the book's likely success. He negotiated a publishing contract with Ernest Hecht's Souvenir Press in London, one of Britain's leading feminist publishers, and Stein & Day in New York City – publishers of Che Guevara, David Frost, and the film director Elia Kazan.[5] Unna's instincts were justified: the *Western Mail* enthused early in 1972 that *The Descent of Woman* was 'expected to earn £100,000' after taking the publishing world by storm.[6] Such a figure, in contemporary terms, would be in excess of £1.3 million.

The American publishing storm was entirely accidental and caused by *Time* magazine's claims in its review of *Descent of Woman* that the book was 'another largely fictional work like Clifford Irving's supposed biography'. The review was unrelenting, suggesting that Elaine's theories were 'even more speculative and sexist than those she decries' and that at best she was 'armed with a vivid imagination and a healthy supply of female chauvinism'.[7] Outraged at the remarks, Elaine's New York publisher, Stein & Day, sued for damages.[8] The stage was set for a remarkable book tour across America, part of which was filmed and made into a television documentary broadcast on the BBC that October (to accompany *Descent of Woman*'s UK release) – amplifying the book's reach.[9] Elaine, meanwhile, benefitted from the revelations surrounding Irving's manufactured biography of the reclusive millionaire and film tycoon, Howard Hughes. That book had been chosen as the May 1972 main selection for the Book of the Month Club until Irving confessed to its fraudulent nature. He was jailed after pleading guilty at his trial that summer. In the scramble to find an alternative, the Club selected *Descent of Woman*.[10] In an interview with the *Guardian*, Ernest Hecht could hardly disguise his delight. 'Elaine Morgan', he stated baldly, 'will be the world best seller of the autumn with "The Descent of Woman"'.[11]

Hype was carefully manipulated by Sol Stein, as Hecht explained to journalists, and helped to extend the book's range and popularity. Behind the scenes, Elaine was by no means a passive observer of the process, nor was she a guided participant as the Hecht interview seemed to imply. Correspondence between Elaine and her publishers, housed at Columbia University in New York City, shows her to have been a shrewd negotiator and self-advocate, aware of the lucrative opportunities which could come from marketing her work to women, especially to members of the women's liberation movement. The extent of her role in shaping *Descent of Woman* into one of the stand-out successes of early 1970s feminist literature can be seen in the changing identity of the book in the months leading up to publication. *Descent of Woman* was not, in fact, the original title of the book: Elaine had submitted her manuscript to Souvenir Press as *The Evolution of Eve* – a name which reflected the instincts and terminology of Elaine's generation of feminists. In the context of then recently published radical feminist texts, such as Germaine Greer's 1970 polemic *The Female Eunuch* or Betty Friedan's pioneering *The Feminist Mystique* (1963), and the growing importance of the women's liberation movement on both sides of the Atlantic, Elaine realised that Eve was 'old fashioned. Especially to the younger generation' and proposed the title change – even insisting.[12] Hecht and Stein were initially sceptical until they realised the commercial potential of a tie-in to the 1971 centenary of Charles Darwin's *The Descent of Man* (1871).

Despite her commercial awareness, Elaine assiduously maintained the image of a 'housewife' which had been her public persona since the start of her scriptwriting career. In interviews her relationship with feminism and liberation were deliberately played down. She had, she told *Life* magazine, characteristically, 'very un libby sort[s] of hobbies' including knitting and pottering in the garden.[13] It was in this vein that the Book of the Month Club offered Elaine's work to its readers. Gilbert Highet, the Scottish-born and Oxford-educated professor of classics at Columbia University, who was a leading judge for the Club, told journalists 'please do not think that this is a loud, angry women's liberation book. On the contrary, it is almost entirely free of the rancour and harshness that darken Kate Millett's *Sexual Politics* and Germaine Greer's *The Female Eunuch*'.[14] Likewise a profile in the *New York Times* depicted Elaine as 'surprisingly moderate when it comes to the women's liberation movement'. She explained to the paper that she 'did her own housework and cooking and had raised her three children by herself'; and that her biggest concern with the more radical edges of women's liberation was that 'a lot are trying to build a movement by hating men'.[15]

Regardless of the realities of authorial presentation, *Descent of Woman* had an immediate impact, reaching number seven on the *New York Times* bestseller list in June 1972.[16] It reached the British

bestseller lists in the autumn.[17] Reviewers were generally supportive, as impressed by the feminist critique of male-orientated
theories of evolution as wary about the scientific basis of the aquatic
ape theory. As the *New York Times* put it:

> Since a number of readers are sure to take Morgan's notions seri-
> ously, she has done a disservice to the very precepts she appears to
> be championing-frankness and honesty in sexual matters, first-class
> citizenship for women and the urgent need for new and creative
> insights into the nature of man. Pseudoscience marches on.[18]

The Canadian novelist Marian Engel, writing in the Toronto-based
Globe and Mail, ignored such concerns and encouraged the public
to 'read it, and if you're a woman, feel something akin to a rush of
relief. Someone has taken on the Tarzanists'.[19] There was a similar
debate in Britain in the autumn of 1972, following initial serialisa-
tion in the *Observer*, and in Australia when the book launched
there in early in 1973.[20] Writing in the London *Times*, Victoria
Brittain suggested that *Descent of Woman* 'is really an essay in
building up feminist pride in our origins' and a demand for 'more
self-respect' for women.[21] Mary Stott echoed that view in the *Daily
Mail*.[22]

Although *Descent of Woman* was the work of an amateur, a
scriptwriter and English literature graduate, rather than a biologist
or anthropologist, scientists and other writers soon began to incor-
porate Elaine's work into their own debates and teaching. Frances
Burton, for example, later professor of anthropology at the University of Toronto, established an evening adult education course
on primate behaviour in Toronto in 1973. The core texts included
Desmond Morris's *The Naked Ape* and Elaine's *Descent of
Woman*.[23] It was within the women's movement that the book
enjoyed its most critical acclaim, despite Elaine being, as she

averred, 'at 52 ... as old as their mothers – and their mothers were regarded as traitors, collaborators with the enemy, having played along with the nuclear-family rigmarole by acquiring a hubby, a few kiddy-winkies, and all that crap'.[24] Indicatively, the Australian feminist writer and activist Dale Spender incorporated *Descent of Woman* into a body of work she labelled 'feminist knowledge' showing how such writing had begun the transformation of academia from 'men's studies' into something far more egalitarian.[25] Likewise the historian and journalist Pat Barr, a member of the Women in Media action group, quoted Elaine approvingly in her 1978 discussion of gender and femininity, *The Framing of the Female*.[26]

But what sort of intervention had Elaine made with *Descent of Woman*? One indication comes from a surviving recording of a radio interview given in the summer of 1972 to the California-based station KPFA.[27] Conducted by Lois Hansen and Julia Curtis, two of KPFA's leading feminist voices, the discussion ranged widely from Elaine's initial motivations in writing the book to female sexuality to the role of gender in human evolution. For the most part, the interview was genial and free-flowing but it broke down as more contentious ideas about women's liberation were engaged. 'Considering the increase with women's liberation and women going into politics and into public life in general', Hansen asked, '[do you think] that there's any hope that women will convince men to alter the rules of their game?' Elaine replied:

> I can't quite see how they're going to do that. I mean, Lionel Tiger
> points out that you have this standard figure of about five percent
> of women who ever rise to the top in politics. And he puts it down
> to all kinds of deficiency ... I think it's really because we are not so
> easily fooled by these mock enemies that are put up, and we are
> not so ready to stick labels on other whole other sections of

humanity. All the same, all the governments and all the political systems that have ever existed so far have been geared to the male mind and the male psyche. I am not at all certain how we are going to ever get to dominate this type of machinery. It seems to me that we've got to find some way of bypassing it altogether.

She admitted that she had had little direct connection with women's liberation groups so far, although she had read about their activities and their commitment to egalitarian approaches to conducting politics. The discussion then moved on to the section of *Descent of Woman* in which Elaine challenged contemporary feminist writing. Hansen began by observing that the chapter said, 'some rather confusing, to me, things about motherhood – you say that animals and old-fashioned and/or lower-class women take great joy in raising children but that many middle-class or liberated women seem to try to want to get rid of their children as often as possible'. Elaine replied that raising children was one of the few processes in modern society that was not subject to 'streamlining' because men took very little interest in the activity of child rearing. 'In the last resort', she concluded, much to the chagrin of her hosts, 'it is we [women] who have got to carry the can ... we choose to have them, we have got the ultimate responsibility for finding some way or other to ensure that they are brought up decently'. Such views were alien to the more radical elements of women's liberation – this was underscored by Carole Dix's review of *Descent of Woman* in the leading British feminist magazine, *Spare Rib*:

Strong Women's Lib, she can't take: any talk of 24 hour nurseries or farming children out, or even a communal set-up where children share parents horrify her. Though she does now agree with abortion on demand.[28]

In the same magazine, Michelene Wandor lamented Elaine's 'snide conviction' that a women's political movement was the wrong approach to improve their lot.[29] Nevertheless, during the 1970s, Elaine was steadily absorbed into the women's movement: her work for the feminist publisher Virago, for instance, brought her into contact with an advisory group which included (amongst others) Germaine Greer, Mary Stott, and Michelene Wandor.

The apparently sudden transformation of Elaine Morgan, the modest fifty-something housewife, into a hero of feminist radicalism was, of course, over-done. Elaine had long been focused on the economic inequalities which impacted most directly on women and much of her best writing for television focused on that field. Yet the success of *Descent of Woman*, and her identification with the women's movement, enabled Elaine to be much bolder and to deal more directly – and overtly – with inequality, feminism, and leftist politics. She got her chance on television and radio, not least in her television play *Liberation Now* (first broadcast in Wales in 1971 and across Britain in 1972) which tackled male ageing and its consequences for women and children and in the two-part *A Woman's Place* in 1978. Likewise, in February 1973, she was invited onto *No Man's Land*, a pioneering women's discussion programme made by Anglia Television and broadcast at the same time as *Match of the Day*. 'A deliberate case of provocation', thought one reviewer.[30] Yet, as the historian Jilly Boyce Kay has noted, this was an important landmark in the public dissemination of the ideas of the women's liberation movement. 'Produced by women who were active in the ... movement; it was presented by the feminist Juliet Mitchell; and its studio audience was populated by, among others, many women who were aligned with the movement'.[31] Elaine was in the same episode as Germaine Greer, invited along to discuss women and sexuality.[32]

In the early 1970s, Elaine appeared on programmes across the BBC and ITV, in fact, not only to talk about her writing but to provide her views on everything from reform to the law on rape to censorship in films to the influence of religion on contemporary society, and, of course, to the evolving status of women in post-war Britain. Whereas Gwyn Thomas, with his appearances on *Parkinson* and the *Vincent Kane Show* in the 1970s seemed to turn himself into the jester, the Welshman who could make everyone laugh, burying his serious points behind jokes; Elaine was the more earnest figure standing up for women's rights, for the rights of children, and for the marginalised in general, with an altogether more serious way of delivering her arguments. Gwyn had similar political leanings, of that there is no doubt, but his was a lighter, comedic touch. Some of these invitations to speak preceded the publication of *Descent of Woman* in Britain in October 1972, but most followed in its wake. It certainly seems unlikely, for example, that Elaine would have been asked to take part in the tenth anniversary broadcast of the BBC Wales programme *Week In, Week Out* in 1974 but for the publication of her book. Even less likely was the excerpting of her work for broadcast on the BBC's Russian Service, which is what happened in November 1972 with *Descent of Woman*.

Newspapers, likewise, offered Elaine opportunities to write op-ed columns, and to make her views known on a range of issues – opinions which were then syndicated around the world. In 1977, she prompted a controversy in the United States with her column 'In Defence of Virgins' which appeared in the *New York Times* at the end of November.[33] Writing in response, one correspondent to the paper's editor, observed sardonically:

> To us the Op-Ed essay by Elaine Morgan...is an unblushingly sub-versive statement. Is this woman intent upon up-ending Freud and

his host of less gods... Does she want to devastate our sex-orientated psychology and educational methodology ... Is she
determined to end our popular literature, or our cinema? ... Such
subversion can be matched only in the political sphere, and those
with lucrative returns from sex-orientated interpretations of life
ought to exile her to the moon.[34]

The response stemmed from Elaine's suggestion that society's
increasingly tolerant attitude to sex might have undesired consequences in presenting sexual abstinence as unvirtuous. 'Those
sections truly progressive', she wrote, 'have by now extended this
degree of tolerance to every sexual minority except one'. She continued: 'the word loosely applied to their alleged deficiency is an
unattractive one. The word is "frigid," and it is a powerful anxiety-
maker'. Of course, the essay was not really about sex but about
Elaine's life-long concern with motherhood and the rearing of
children. She wrote,

> We have this arbitrary conviction that, if you have the biological
> capacity to do something and yet don't want to do it, then you are
> "inhibiting" your deepest instincts, and this must be bad. But recent
> developments have shown that this is a very dubious argument.
>
> For example, practically all women have the biological capacity
> to produce and rear children, and possibly 90 percent of them also
> have the urge to do so. But we have lately had many reminders –
> some of them harsh – that not all women do want to have children,
> and not all women who have them want to look after them, and
> if conditions compel them to do so, the babies sometimes end up
> battered in hospital and the mothers in jail – even though the
> maternal instinct is quite as powerful and ancient and deep rooted
> as the sexual one.

In Wales, Elaine stood out as a lone voice. The 1970s were a decade
– following the retirement of Eirene White from the East Flintshire

seat in 1970 – when Wales had no women representatives in West-minster. Only the election of Ann Clwyd as a member of the European parliament in 1979 masked the complete absence of women in the upper echelons of Welsh politics. So much so that in 1979, it was Elaine who was invited on to discussion programmes to debate devolution alongside male politicians. Her status had been confirmed in 1975, during the UN's International Year of Women, when she received the invitation to deliver the annual radio lecture for BBC Radio Wales, the first woman ever to be asked. The lecture was broadcast on 10 November 1975, a few days after Elaine's 55th birthday. She chose *Women and Society* as her title and wondered when it would be possible for the Welsh to sing about hen *wlad fy mamau*; considered the need for greater legal protections for chil-dren; and the potential implications of the Equal Pay Act. The legislation had been passed by the Labour government in 1970 and was due to come into force on 29 December 1975.[35]

What followed Elaine's lecture – behind the scenes, at least – was a proposed thirteen-part series for BBC Wales, *Ascent of Woman*, which would have provided a feminist alternative to doc-umentaries made in earlier years by Desmond Morris and others. It got as far as a sample script but was not taken further. Similar examples of programmes which made the development phase but which were not, in the end, produced included an adaptation of Jan Morris's memoir *Conundrum* for BBC Wales in 1985, a multi-part biographical serial on the life of Mother Theresa at around the same time, a four-part series based on Ivor Novello's *The Dancing Years,* and a three part series based on *Helbeck of Bannisdale* by the Victorian novelist Mary Augusta Ward. Whereas Elaine's prominence as a writer and commentator on the experi-ences of women, past and present, was assured, regardless of the success or failure of scripts such as these, the other themes of

Elaine's career – not least environmentalism, materialist consumption, and what is now known as global warming – did not make the impact that they should have done. In part this was because of timing – had Elaine's work appeared around the same time as President Jimmy Carter's 'Moral Equivalent of War' speech, about the burgeoning energy crisis, given in April 1977, she might had added to the zeitgeist. As it was, her work appeared six months earlier with far less public attention.

Falling Apart: The Rise and Decline of Urban Civilization, Elaine's follow up to the *Descent of Woman* appeared in late October 1976. Published by Souvenir Press in the UK, Methuen in Canada, and Stein & Day in the United States, it 'sank without trace'. As Elaine recalled, she felt this was because 'I bit off more than I could chew'. Certainly, it has continued to be overshadowed by the on-going impact of *Descent of Woman*, and never reprinted, but this was not an entirely fair judgement of a work readily identifiable as a proto-environmentalist classic. A favourable review by Peter Lewis in the *Daily Mail* encouraged that the book 'should be placed on every city planner and administrator's desk'.[36] *Falling Apart* was also translated into several European languages including Catalan, Dutch, and Spanish. Read in the early twenty first century, the book's central message that, left to its own devices, London would become a city of the very rich, the very old, and the very poor, and would become dysfunctional, has more than a ring of truth. At the time, of course, defenders of continuous metropolitan and urban expansion at the expense of the countryside and the industrial periphery were in the ascendancy and Elaine faced a difficult time presenting her ideas on radio and television.[37]

Falling Apart reflected Elaine's deep absorption in Marxist ideas and her own historic commitments to the anti-nuclear proliferation and peace campaigns, which brought her into contact with the emerging ecology movement in Britain as well as the eco-socialist left – including within Plaid Cymru and the Communist Party. The book was her plea for a better set of decisions on the world's future and drew on the new economic ideas of writers such as Leopold Kohr (who was then teaching at Aberystwyth) and E.F. Schumacher, both of whom had been active in forging the 'small is beautiful' model of development.[38] In the aftermath of the 1973-74 energy crisis, and with the looming threat of another, which eventually occurred in 1979, Elaine wondered whether humans would make the right choice between saving the planet and continuing to expand a throw-away culture. 'Today', she wrote in *Falling Apart*, 'there seems to be at least an even chance that the world may not after all be travelling down that poisonous road, but may choose a cleaner and greener one'.[39] More than forty years later, it is self-evident that consumerism won all the same. Underpinning Elaine's ideas in *Falling Apart* were works by leading Marxist intellectuals including the geographer David Harvey, historian Eric Hobsbawm, and literary critic Raymond Williams, together with Karl Marx's own *Das Kapital* and works by Kohr and Schumacher. This was hardly the typical reading fare of the housewife, but indicative of a background in adult education.

There were obvious parallels between *Falling Apart* and Desmond Morris's own sequel to *The Naked Ape*. Published in 1969, and serialised in the *Daily Mirror*, *The Human Zoo* contended that urban society, particularly life in cities, had many of the characteristics of a zoo. Humans, like animals, had their basic needs provided for but were forced out of their natural habitat as a result. Thus, they develop less healthy relationships and suffer from social diseases such as loneliness, isolation, and boredom. Flats and houses of multiple occupation evoked similar ideas to the cages of a zoo. Civilisation had evolved to provide 'coping mechanisms',

which had undoubtedly encouraged tremendous growth, intellec-
tually and scientifically, but this 'adaptation' also came with other
costs and prompted other problems, not least war and sexual crime.
Morris's argument proved controversial on first publication, but
journalists were no less able to present it as a text with strong appeal
to housewives and others who 'anxiously' sought copies in their
local library.[40] It is possible, although unlikely given the absence of
reference to Morris's work (Elaine was generally honest in that
regard), that Elaine modelled *Falling Apart* on *The Human Zoo* –
the common themes were there as was the warning that humanity
might well be on its way to self-exhaustion.

In this case, however, it was Kohr and Schumacher who inspired
Elaine and in the years after the publication of *Falling Apart*, she
became a regular contributor to and reviewer for several of the
leading magazines of the British ecology movement (the forerunner
of the Green Party of England and Wales) including *Resurgence*
and *The New Ecologist*.[41] Kohr wrote an approving review of
Elaine's book for *Resurgence* early in 1977, concluding that it was
'a top rate argument in favour of devolution', and in the summer
of 1978, *The New Ecologist* republished an excerpt from *Falling
Apart* for its special on 'revitalising the city'.[42] Together with original articles on cities and a response to the oil crisis of 1979, in
which she warned about the dangers of swapping fossil fuels for
nuclear energy, Elaine earned for herself a place within the canon
of ecological writing from the period. Although she would later
insist that *Falling Apart* had been a relative failure, Elaine was
prominent enough within the ecology movement at the time to
warrant being part of the E.F. Schumacher Memorial Foundation
which was launched in November 1977. She served as a sponsor,
together with the violinist Yehudi Menuhin and the green cam-
paigners Edward Goldsmith and Gerard Morgan-Grenville.[43]

Disappointed, perhaps, that her efforts in the field of ecology had not had the same impact as her earlier work on evolution and feminism, Elaine returned in the early 1980s to the ideas present in *Descent of Woman*. Although the aquatic ape theory had been an underlying part of her 1972 book, it had been somewhat over-shadowed by the attention attracted by the book's feminist spirit. 'I began to realize', Elaine wrote, 'that by putting the aquatic theory into the same book as the feminism ... I had made it too easy for the pundits to dismiss it out of hand without needing to give their reasons'. She started to work on a sequel, wherein the aquatic case could be set out in such a way as to be less easy to 'brush aside'. It appeared in March 1982 as *The Aquatic Ape*.[44] The volume con-sidered three approaches to human evolution − the savannah, the neotenic (which was the most recent and referred to the retention of juvenile features into adulthood), and the aquatic − and incor-porated Alister Hardy's papers on the aquatic ape theory into the text. This was a determined − although initially not entirely suc-cessful − effort to transform what had been a feminist retort into a scientific one. *The Aquatic Ape* did, however, lead to a revival of interest in *Descent of Woman*, which was reissued in a revised edition in 1985. A string of publications in popular magazines such as the *New Scientist* likewise followed, as did a high-profile con-ference in Valkenberg in the Netherlands in 1987.[45]

Towards the end of the 1980s, at a time when Elaine's work for television and radio was coming to an end, her involvement in the scientific debates on human evolution began to intensify. In 1990, Souvenir Press published Elaine's third book, *The Scars of Evolu-tion*, an attempt to (as the blurb put it) 'solve one of the enduring riddles of our origins' and to 'discover the evolutionary path that separated us from the rest of the animals'. In doing so, she drew attention to all the areas of human evolution that seemed to have gone wrong – back pain, obesity, acne, and even varicose veins – but which were in fact, she argued, apt responses to problems that humans had to confront to survive. As evidence of Elaine's increasing scientific presence, at least for a lay audience, *The Scars of Evolution* was the first of her books to be issued by a major publisher in paperback – Penguin won the rights in the UK and Oxford University Press (OUP) in the United States. A similar situation prevailed with Elaine's fourth book in her series on evolutionary biology and human pre-history, *The Descent of the Child*, which was first published by Souvenir Press in 1994. Neither Penguin nor OUP, however, were involved with *The Aquatic Ape Hypothesis,* which appeared in 1997.[46]

The early 1990s brought celebrity friends and fans to Elaine's work on anthropology, not least the scriptwriter and novelist Douglas Adams and, for a time, his close friend the biologist and evolutionist Richard Dawkins.[47] Adams was, in Elaine's words, a 'mad fan' and introduced her to the internet. In the United States, she was feted by the philosopher Daniel Dennett, another of Dawkins's friends, who promoted Elaine's work in his 1995 book *Darwin's Dangerous Idea.* Perhaps the most significant encouragement came, however, from David Attenborough whom Elaine had first met in 1979 when commissioned to interview him for the *Radio Times* ahead of the broadcast of the ground-breaking documentary *Life on Earth.* Attenborough's intervention, in his capacity as the annual president of the British Association for the Advancement of Science, enabled a panel on the aquatic ape theory to be presented at the British Science Festival in Southampton in the summer of 1992.[48] A decade later, Attenborough included the theory in his 2002 documentary series, *The Life of Mammals,* and presented a two-part radio series in 2005 called *The Scars of Evolution* – the title clearly paying homage to Elaine's earlier work.

Each programme served to increase public awareness of her ideas, and of her contribution to evolutionary science.

Given all this activity, and her retirement from scriptwriting in 1989, it is easy to forget that Elaine turned seventy in 1990 and eighty in 2000 – the year she was awarded the Norwegian Letten F. Saugstad Prize for her contributions to scientific knowledge. That in her eighth decade she was travelling to Scandinavia, the United States, and South Africa, as well as all over Britain, presenting at conferences and engaging in rich intellectual debate, was a remarkable feat. More so given that this was a field in which she had no professional qualification – although this did not go unnoticed in the scientific community and she was not wholly welcomed. In the early years of the new millennium, and following Morien's death aged eighty-one in 1997, Elaine did begin to slow down. Morien's passing, after more than half a century of marriage, was a blow which might have led to an ordinary twilight: the peaceful end of one's own generation. But it was not to be. Elaine certainly wrote less frequently to begin with, concentrating her efforts on short autobiographical pieces for edited volumes such as those published by the Welsh women's press, Honno, and her memoir *Knock 'Em Cold, Kid,* which appeared in 2012. Her final scientific writings were self-published: *Pinker's List* in 2005 and *The Naked Darwinist* in 2008.

In addition to writing, Elaine became an in-demand figure at public events, and she enjoyed a period of unusual richness and public renown and won a raft of awards and titles including a lifetime achievement award from BAFTA Cymru in 2003. Thus, in 2001 she participated in the launch of the social justice think tank, the Bevan Foundation; in 2005 she was interviewed about her life by veteran broadcaster Mavis Nicholson (who came out of retirement for the occasion); and was the star attraction at the Women's

Archive of Wales roadshow in Pontypridd in 2009. In 2006, she was awarded an honorary doctorate by the University of Glamorgan and made an honorary fellow of Cardiff University the following year. An OBE was awarded in 2009, as was fellowship of the Royal Society of Literature. But these were retrospectives, awards granted for achievements over a long-life of significant achievement – they did not change Elaine's life so much as reflect what she had previously done. Then one day, early in 2003, a letter arrived at Elaine's home in Aberffrwd Road in Mountain Ash. It contained a striking offer from the editor of the *Western Mail* – an invitation to write a weekly column to be published in the Friday edition. Having harboured a life-long ambition to become a journalist and keen to continue to put pen to paper, Elaine readily agreed. She set retirement aside to become 'The Pensioner'.

SEVEN
THE PENSIONER

Elaine was eighty-two when she began writing her weekly column for the *Western Mail* and one of the oldest columnists anywhere in Britain – her old friend Rose Hacker, who wrote for the *Camden New Journal* as a centenarian, was the oldest. Long since retired from scriptwriting but still embroiled in debates about the aquatic ape theory, it was *The Pensioner* which brought Elaine to the attention of a new audience, particularly amongst younger generations, and afforded, in the last years of her life, the title of 'national treasure'. In the early days of the column, ideas were (to borrow the words of Trevor Fishlock) hatched during morning walks and polished into a column of around five hundred words by Tuesday for publication each Friday. 'In my column', Elaine was to reflect, 'I thought I was writing so much common sense. I thought I would hit everybody in the eye (with it)'. The prototype appeared in the *Western Mail* on 31 January 2003. It was all about old age and life expectancy, and began

> The Bible said we should live to 70 years of age – three score years and 10 – though it is not clear whether that average included special cases like Methuselah .... Buthese days you don't know where you are. We had hardly got used to life expectancy going up to 75, before it had shot up again to 80. I am now 82, an age when people who bump into you are apt to register slight surprise, as if they were thinking "Odd! You still here, then?"[1]

This was a characteristically conversational opening to a series remembered for its charm and homeliness, but which contained more than a few political barbs aimed directly at the New Labour government which Elaine felt had begun to lose some of the idealism with which it had first entered office six years earlier. Column two tackled public and personal debt and the question of spending.[2] Number three focused on teaching and the decline in public appreciation of the role of the educator, and the significance of schools and universities. It deserves quoting in full, illustrating Elaine's continued disguise of her own career as a teacher and lecturer.

My personal experience of teaching was brief and undistinguished. But I was married for more than fifty years to a true professional – the French master at what used to be the Pontypridd Boys' Grammar School. He never talked much to me about his work. By the end of a day at the chalk face, he needed to take his mind off it. So I only learned how good he was from the many people who came up to me and said, in the early days, "I know your husband – he's teaching my son" and, in later years, "Yes, I knew Morien. He taught me". They all praised him, many said he had made a difference to their lives. This is what teaching is all about. At one time it was the most prestigious job you could aspire to in the Welsh Valleys, and teachers were held in the highest esteem. Every vacant post in the schools was hotly competed for. Now we learn that thirty per cent of those in the profession are counting the days until they can get out. What changed?

Society changed. Education's raw material is children, and they have certainly changed. At any given age they are bigger than we were, and the age for the onset of puberty is going down all the time. Parents and teachers used to be their only source of information about the wider world, but now they have direct access to all the media (God help them), from radio to cyberspace. Today's child of 16 may feel as resentful of being stuck in a classroom as his grandfather would have been at 20. In the rawest sectors of the educational world, one such resentful pupil can wreck a classroom – and you can't lay a finger on him. In more fortunate areas, the children may be receptive and the job itself still rewarding. Yet even in those schools, many teachers are voting with their feet because of the harassment imposed by the ministerial determination to "modernise".

In the commercial world, modernising means streamlining and cost-cutting by improving business management, introducing automation, and fragmenting production into simpler processes requiring less skill. Thus the actual producers on the shop floor are fewer and more readily replaceable and the end product cheaper and more uniform. More and better management is the magic key. That will never work where the end product is a human being. You cannot replace doctors and nurses and teachers by machines. You cannot deconstruct their relationship with pupils and patients into bite-sized chunks that can be mindlessly carried out by anybody after a week's training.

It is excellent news that the Government is spending more money on the public services, but we need to keep an eye on the ratio between how much of it goes on administration, inspection, and documentation, and how much is spent on the people at the sharp end. "Education... Education... Education" was a splendid slogan, but it needs to be made more concrete. The highest priority needs to be focused on "The teachers... The teachers... The teachers."[3]

Soon there were columns about sex, ageing, women's liberation, the Iraq War, social change, Welshness, and the discomfort the elderly feel in a world that has transformed around them. These were precisely the topics which editors had anticipated, and which readers enjoyed. Read from a distance, however, and with a more careful consideration of the contents, *The Pensioner* can (and should) be seen both as a carefully setting out of the deeper truths of Elaine's own life and, in a final act of holding up the mirror, as a chronicle of Blair's Britain. A rather unflattering one at that. One feisty column, published to mark the twentieth anniversary of the 1984-85 miners' strike, carried the headline 'lessons from the past for our messianic leader'. It was, of course, only marginally about the miners or their industrial disputes from two decades before and had more to say about the increasingly presidential style of leadership which Elaine saw (and disliked) in the prime minister, Tony Blair.[4] 'I have', she reflected, 'fond memories of Clem Attlee, a comparatively self effacing figure. His method seemed to be that he listened carefully to what his people wanted, and searched for practical ways of giving it to them. There are worse ways of running a political party'.[5]

Labour won its third general election in 2005 (it has yet to win another). In the months leading up to the poll, Elaine used her column to push for Tony Blair to stand down as leader of the Labour Party and allow 'a new rising star ... who will remind us of some of the reasons why it came into existence in the first place'.[6] It was a call to pull Labour to the left once more and to rescind the apparent vow to make the Conservatives unelectable by ensuring that 'whatever the cost, never again shall any political party outflank Labour on the right'. As she put it, 'that's an unnecessarily high price to pay'. The result of that decision, which Elaine recognised but did not live to see, was the rise of voter apathy (in some cases) and disengagement (in others), and a populism (left and right) which has ultimately destabilised British politics. Her columns in this period stand as the initial diagnosis and deserve thusly to be read. In April 2005, with the poll having been declared and parliament dissolved, she wrote

> Nobody seems to doubt the outcome of the May election. Sup-
> porters of the Labour Party should be in a state of euphoria,

looking forward to the victory celebrations following their third victory in a row. But in roughly sixty five years as a party member I have never known a time when there was less enthusiasm for that prospect.[7]

The problem, as Elaine saw it, was Tony Blair, who (in her view) had misjudged the country in engaging in the Iraq War and had misjudged the Labour Party and its membership by not moving to the left.[8] Elaine continued, the note of despair evident in her words,

> I can't conceive of voting for any other party, but for the first time I can conceive of not voting at all, and it won't be out of apathy. Even after Iraq, I have kept hoping against hope that Tony Blair would begin to show a glimmer of understanding of why so many people in his own party begin to despair of him. He recently had a chance to appease our anxieties by giving an interview to the [centre-right] Labour journal, Progress. He was asked about his 2001 statement that he was not worried about the growing gap between rich and poor. He incidentally described himself as "one of the least politically correct people in Britain". I can understand why [Robert] Kilroy-Silk would regard that as a matter for pride, but I'm afraid I cannot vote for a Labour leader who sees it as something to boast about.

Kilroy-Silk, a former member of the Labour shadow cabinet, had been elected to the European Parliament in 2004 as a member of the United Kingdom Independence Party, leaving in 2005 to form the hard-line anti-immigration party Veritas.

In the event, Elaine abstained from voting in part 'because Tony Blair's activities had immovably stuck in my gullet'.[9] But equally because she held out some hope that the post-election rancour between the Blairites and Brownites might settle down into a change of vocabulary bringing the 'dissidents back on board for a few more years' – herself included. For her part, Elaine looked for reassurance that concessions from the Labour leadership were forthcoming and that dissent in the party would be looked upon more favourably. As she put it, 'joining a political party does not involve swearing a lifetime allegiance to "my leader right or wrong"'.[10] Elaine was soon disappointed. The public debate about the appropriate response to terrorism, about detention without charge, the on-going conflicts in Iraq and Afghanistan, and the newspeak of the War on Terror with its evocation of an Orwellian nightmare, dissolved any remaining enthusiasm she had for New Labour. In a column published at the end of July 2005, she was strident:

> Personally, I am unwilling to pay the price of losing a citizen's right not to be kept under arrest for ever-lengthening periods without even being told what the charge is. That is not the British way of life we are being called on to defend. It's a police state policy. The principle of habeas corpus has survived eight hundred turbulent years of British history... When I am asked to watch it being snuffed out on account of a small bunch of fanatics in 2005, I regard that as a wake-up call. Various chunks of our civil liberties have been quietly binned already ... During the last war some of our liberties were curtailed "for the duration". We knew the war would end one day and we would get them back. However the "war on terror" is different. No one but the government will have any say in deciding when it suits them to declare it is over. They are already preparing us to accept that it will go on like this for decades, so that our children could grow up without any memory of what it used to be like to live in a free country.[11]

Towards the end of 2005, Elaine was invited by the Cynon Valley Constituency Labour Party to deliver its annual Keir Hardie Memorial Lecture. Her theme was 'Old Labour and New Labour'. Elaine laid out her concerns to party members about the apparent 'civil war bursting out in your own back yard'.[12] As she was to write almost a year later, 'more and more, party members have been telling him [Blair] he's leading them in a direction they don't want to go, but he wasn't listening. He's convinced that anyone disagreeing with him must be stupid or ignorant'. It was at that moment, in September 2006, that Elaine predicted that Labour would go on to lose the next general election. 'Could it be condemned to a spell in the wilderness?' she wondered, 'Yes, I'm afraid it could'. Adding that

> I don't know how to say this, but by now I can't really care much one way or the other. The difference between what the two parties are offering seems paper thin. Besides, I suspect this period of hot-house growth fuelled by US deficit budgets and spiralling private debt is bound to run into the buffers before long ... A few years of slim-down economics, instead of 'affluenza' – the overstuffed consumption mania of the last few years – might lead to really constructive new thinking. It won't be popular though. And I can't help asking myself: which party would I like to be in office when the crunch comes?[13]

Elaine's prescient column was published almost exactly twelve months before the beginning of the credit crisis at the Northern Rock bank in September 2007. What Elaine was describing was the likely effect of a financial downturn and a further wave of economic malaise. 'I've long been interested in the tensions between great metropolitan cities and the people who live far away from them', she wrote later, once the true effects of the banking crisis had become clear, 'ever since [political theorist, economist, and Labour Party chairman] Harold Laski described it as one of the problems created by unfettered capitalism'.[14] Elaine continued,

> It tends, he said, to generate "apoplexy at the centre and anaemia at the extremities." This problem has become more acute as Britain

becomes more dependent on the financial sector to keep the country solvent. Now, with the banks in crisis, there are some signs that the magnetic force attracting people to the South East may be slackening. ... You may ask: 'why should we worry about London's problems, when we have plenty of our own?' Because it could become our problem too. Cardiff Bay has a lot in common with London's Canary Wharf. The gap in earnings, house prices, and living costs between Cardiff and, for example, the Valleys has been rising fast.

She warned readers that,

> In Wales we've tended to pride ourselves on this bourgeoning: it proves we're just as good at conspicuous consumption as anybody else, when we put our minds to it. It would be sad if it turned out that we learned to play the game just when it was turning out to be the wrong game.

Tony Blair eventually stood down in the summer of 2007 leaving Gordon Brown in Downing Street. 'We won't see any miracles', Elaine warned, by now convinced of the looming economic down-turn, 'the scale of the problems ahead is daunting and Gordon's shackled by the necessity of not moving faster than the electorate will let him. But I believe he may be the best hope, not only for Labour but for the country too'.[15] It was not, of course, how it turned out. A few weeks after Gordon Brown's succession to the premiership, the financial crisis that Elaine had predicted a year earlier came to pass. She turned over her column in the *Western Mail* to the everyday effects of what was going on. In November 2007, she pondered an intellectual debate she had had with the then chairman of Northern Rock in her book *Pinker's List*. 'He dislikes governments, environmentalists, and anyone who wants to limit the freedom of private enterprise', she noted, before landing her blow: 'and when the angry crowds were queueing outside the bank, was he tempted to go out and explain how the magic hand of the market had lost its magic, and their only hope lay in appealing to the nasty old government?'[16]

Of Brown's Conservative opponent, David Cameron, she was scathing. Cameron, she wrote in 2009, 'sounds like King Lear: "I will do such things – what they are yet I know not – but they shall be the terrors of the earth!"'.[17] Her portrait was even less flattering in the run up to the 2010 general election:

> There's something so vapid about that guy. He thinks he's leading his party. He's not leading anybody. He's just standing in front of them, saying: 'it's all going to be different and we're not nearly as nasty as we used to be' – but nobody's following him, not even the ones who think they can understand what he's saying. They're using him as a fig leaf, hoping he'll open the door of Number Ten for them and once they're in, they'll tell him what he's got to do. It'll be the same as it always was ... He's saying in effect: 'vote for me and it'll be just like having Tony back'. Thanks a bunch, Dave: we have been warned. I'm going to vote Labour to keep the Tories out. It's not the most heart-stirring of slogans. But to quote Shakespeare just once more: ''tis enough. 'Twill serve'.[18]

During the first two years of the coalition government led by David Cameron, Elaine felt vindicated in her earlier judgement that he was a politician not to be trusted. The prime minister, she wrote in 2011, 'instinctively senses the growing element of class conflict in today's society, and is not afraid to indicate whose side he's on' adding that 'he has subtly begun to demonise the unemployed as the chief authors of their own plight'.[19] Elaine was as forthright in her criticism of the Coalition as of New Labour, although her advancing age meant *The Pensioner* was less robust in the 2010s than it had been in the 2000s. Nevertheless, she persisted with the column and it stands as a significant commentary on the early twenty-first century from an important voice of the twentieth.

In fact, many of Elaine's columns, and those she occasionally contributed to newspapers such as the *Guardian*, which were not about contemporary politics dealt with issues such as climate change, identity, and gender, which make them seem prophetic when read retrospectively. Her response to the parliamentary expenses scandal pointed to the increasingly avaricious nature of modern politicians. 'If you go back to 1945', she wrote, 'and imagine a *News of the World* reporter trying to bribe or blackmail, say, Bessie Braddock or Nye Bevan, it's very hard to believe they'd have rolled over. They had too much fire in their bellies'.[20] But Elaine was not given over entirely to nostalgia, or to the lessons of the past, she retained a clear focus on the present and the future. She even signed up for Twitter, describing the bewildering and ultimately frustrating experience in a column in February 2010:

> I'd never twittered anything before but I pressed various keys and was offered a form to fill in. You simply have to invent a username and a password, and type them in. It's simple. You just choose something easy for you to remember. I typed in my maiden surname – Floyd. The computer said that username was already taken. Ok, my mother's maiden name – Neville. Already taken. My grandmother's maiden name: Rendall. Already taken. (Sigh) I got clever and typed in Ynysybwl.[21]

After a few more minutes fighting with the signup system, she gave up, preferring instead to stick with the printed word. 'And even if I do say it myself, she remarked sardonically, 'I'm no slouch at the printed word'. All that in her ninetieth year.

2011 was a tragic one for Elaine, despite her on-going success as a columnist. Dylan, her eldest son, passed away suddenly in early

March. She wrote about him in *The Pensioner*, bringing back to her own memory various incidents that punctuated both their lives. There was Dylan the actor, Dylan the chess player, and Dylan the scientist. She wrote:

> There was the time when he travelled around places like Dublin to play in chess tournaments, or the time when he went to Leningrad, and the period when there was opencast mining just behind our bungalow in Abernant, and he would follow in the wake of the "walking dragline", looking for fossils in the newly exposed deposits.[22]

There was also the son who was humble in his achievements, who followed in his parents' footsteps but charted his own course. She reflected:

> [Dylan] never had the slightest interest in being famous. I'm sure ifhe could read this he'd protest that I've gone way over the top with those superlatives. But I didn't make them up. And they're helping me to realise how fulfilling his life was and how much he enjoyed it.

Elaine experienced profound grief at Dylan's early death. As she explained in her memorial column: 'For a couple of weeks I had no curiosity at all about what was going on in the world outside, and when I did start opening newspapers again I almost wished I hadn't'. She carried on writing for the *Western Mail* though, and a year later was awarded 'Columnist of the Year' at the Regional Press Awards. The judges declared her work to be 'a genuinely unique voice ... beautifully crafted and laced with wit, self knowledge and wisdom'.[23] It was a valedictory statement.

Elaine's final column was published that summer, a few weeks after a mini stroke which meant that she could no longer fully manage the task of writing. She wrote honestly and movingly about its effects.[24] Her penultimate submission, characteristic of the political fortitude she had displayed in a decade as a columnist, was about the on-going Greek financial crisis.[25] But, under the headline 'after 2012's brouhaha, I've a great 2013 ahead of me', Elaine's column ended abruptly on 15 June 2012. As she endeavoured to recover from a more serious stroke, announced properly in an interview in August 2012, *The Pensioner* was replaced with extracts from her autobiography before her retirement was announced in January 2013 – ten years exactly from her first appearance.[26] Retirement brought with it a flurry of new awards – including the Freedom of the County Borough of Rhondda Cynon Taff – and a testimonial documentary broadcast in March 2013.[27] The then chair of the Arts Council of Wales, Dai Smith, observed of Elaine that she was 'always, I think from the beginning, exceptional ... I have a sense of this little girl, Elaine Floyd, in these streets, observing things, looking at things. In a way it's as if she's always been an observer'.[28]

She was, also, a willing provocateur when it came to evolution, and towards the very end of her life Elaine enjoyed a new kind of celebrity – that of internet lecturer and YouTube sensation. Celebration of Charles Darwin's bicentennial in 2009 provided a final opportunity to present the case for the aquatic ape theory. In October 2008, Elaine delivered a seminar at University College London and in February 2009 she lectured in Shrewsbury, Darwin's birthplace, on the theme of 'how we became human'. Each of these lectures and seminars was, in effect, a preamble to perhaps the most remarkable – certainly the most popular – lecture she ever gave, a TED talk delivered in Oxford in July 2009 as part of the 'curious and curiouser' conference panel. Viewed more than a million times since publication online, despite on-going criticisms of the theory,

Elaine's feisty and spirited presentation added to her appeal. Since most of her writing was, by then, and except for *Descent of Woman*, out of print, her appearance online provided an important glimpse into her ideas, particularly for younger generations. One last chapter on the theory, in a fiftieth anniversary collection of essays on Alister Hardy, was published in 2011.[29]

Elaine died, following a final stroke, at Prince Charles Hospital, Merthyr Tydfil, on 12 July 2013. She was ninety two. Her death was reported widely and the tributes warm. Peter Stead, historian and broadcaster, remarked that 'she was a very, very formidable figure and a genuine hero and she was a Welsh great ... [who] kept alive the flame of idealism that existed in the valleys'. In her tribute, columnist Carolyn Hitt, remembered that 'I didn't have to look very far for a role model. Just to the next valley, in fact, where Elaine Morgan changed the world from her desk in Mountain Ash'. She continued

> I particularly loved Elaine's writing style — direct, spare, con-
> versational and punchy. That's why her television characters
> leapt into life from her scripts and her Western Mail columns
> left readers feeling they were engaged in a stimulating one-to-
> one chat. I loved her wisdom too ... Those of us with similar
> backgrounds have been told by the ignorant and the patronising
> that being a valley girl can hold us back. But Elaine said her
> roots were precisely the reason she succeeded. And she never
> left them behind.[30]

The radio broadcaster, Roy Noble, who delivered an address at Elaine's funeral which was held on 25 July 2013 at Llwydcoed Crematorium near Aberdare, similarly remarked on her significance for the people of the South Wales Valleys. 'She was', he said, 'an extraordinary woman. Her intellect was fathoms deep, but she looked and sounded very valleys and she was one of us. We need icons and flag bearers from the valleys to show who we are'.[31] The crematorium chapel was filled with family, the famous, and well-wishers from across the many spheres with which Elaine had an association. It was, befitting the woman who had applied to an Anglican college at Oxford and written 'no religion' when asked her faith, a humanist service during which friends and family shared their recollections, but from which religion was absent. Poems which she had loved were read out and songs were sung or played. Amongst them Paul Robeson's *Old Man River* and Andrea Bocelli's *Time to Say Goodbye*.[32]

★ ★ ★

Few people born in the South Wales Coalfield in the twentieth century enjoyed a career like that which Elaine Morgan built for herself. In many respects she was utterly unique: an inimitability evident as early as 1939 when she became the first pupil from Pontypridd Intermediate School for Girls to go up to Oxford. The only other Welsh girl at Lady Margaret Hall during Elaine's time there was wealthy enough to have had elocution lessons to mask her Welsh origins. Elaine had no such polishing in Pontypridd. That she was once identified as having precisely the character to serve as a Labour member of parliament ought not to be surprising; nor, indeed, was her commitment to environmentalism, nuclear disarmament, adult education, and the Welsh language. In her long life she worked with many of the most famous actors, directors, producers, presenters, and television and radio executives, household names as varied as David Attenborough, Stanley Baker, Jessie Evans, Philip and Ruth Madoc, Julia Sawalha, and Sian Phillips. In the

BBC documentary on Elaine's life broadcast in the spring of 2013, Dai Smith observed that

> If we look at the path of Elaine Morgan's life, I'm sure of one thing. That from the off there was a steely core to it. She was energetic, she was ambitious, and she did what she wanted to do. She got an education in Pontypridd and in Oxford. She did write. She became, in a sense, that journalist that the little girl had said she wanted to become. And I think that's a tremendous achievement. She is a great, great exemplar, actually of what Hopkinstown would have wanted her to be all those years ago.

Half a century earlier, journalist Brinley Evans had said something similar. Elaine Morgan, he wrote, added

> a shining record of service to the working class and no-one has portrayed with a surer touch the short and simple annals of the poor in our mining villages.[33]

Elaine Morgan, like her near contemporaries Gwyn Thomas, Alun Richards, and Ron Berry, did indeed fulfil the twentieth century South Walian dream. Over the course of her long life, she experienced and bore witness to the transformation of the proletarian universality of the coalfield into which she was born into a post-industrial society. One defined as much by the absence of opportunities and popular disengagement with politics as by the faint echoes of the radical past. She ensured, through her writing for television and radio that the voices and experiences of valleys women were included in the historical record, and through her scientific writing that the role of women in human evolution could not be dismissed. Never again will science automatically assert that Eve followed in Adam's wake. In the end, Elaine's life had been turned by education, which lasted for as long as she chose, from poverty into opportunity. Alongside Gwyn Thomas, she helped to define what Wales meant for television and radio audiences all over the world. Whether as the pensioner, the playwright, the protester, the poet's muse, or the student politician, Elaine was determined to say to her own community, to her own people, first and foremost, it does not have to be this way.

NOTES

Introduction

1 Angela John, *Rocking the Boat: Welsh Women Who Championed Equality, 1840-1990* (Cardigan: Parthian, 2018).

2 Elaine Morgan is, for instance, absent from Katie Gramich's survey *Twentieth-Century Women's Writing in Wales: Land, Gender, Belonging* (Cardiff: University of Wales Press, 2007).

3 *The Stage*, 13 May 1982.

4 Nicola Davies, 'Elaine Morgan', *New Welsh Review* 2, no. 1 (Summer 1989), 31.

5 Donald Wilson, 'Foreword: You're A Long Time Dead by Elaine Morgan', in Michael Barry (ed.), *The Television Playwright* (London: Michael Joseph, 1960), 349.

6 Robert Bowen was born in Coalbrook Vale, Monmouthshire, on 11 December 1909. A talented artist and active member of the Primitive Methodist church, Bowen graduated from Balliol College with first class honours in 1931. Returning to South Wales, he became an English teacher in Nantyglo and Newbridge before becoming County Librarian for Monmouthshire in 1933. Bowen died suddenly in March 1937. *Western Mail*, 21 June 1927, 30 March 1937, *Methodist Leader*, 30 June 1927; Evo Elliot (ed), *Balliol College Register* (Oxford: Balliol College, 1953), 278.

7 Elaine Morgan, 'The Pensioner', 16 September 2011.

8 Edwards was born in Ogmore Vale in 1902. She took her own life in 1934. Her novel *Winter Sonata* and short story collection *Rhapsody* were reissued in 1986 by Virago with forewords by Elaine Morgan.

9 Although she did briefly teach at Pontypridd Girls' Grammar School. *The Magazine of the County Grammar School for Girls, Pontypridd*, 1963, 7.

10 Elaine Morgan, 'Foreword', in Gwyn Thomas, *The Dark Philosophers* (Cardigan, 2006 edn.), xii.

Chapter 1

1 Elaine Morgan, *Knock 'Em Cold Kid* (London, 2012), 9. The unusual street name commemorated the British victory at the battle of Tel-El-Kebir in Egypt

in 1882.

2 *Western Mail*, 2 March 2013.

3 *Western Mail*, 4 April 1956.

4 Gwyn Thomas, 'Foreword', in *Old Pontypridd and District in Photographs* (Barry: Stewart Williams, 1977).

5 As above.

6 E.J. Griffiths, *Medical Officer of Health Report, 1925* (Pontypridd, 1925), 11.

7 *Western Mail*, 29 April 1870.

8 Eleanor died there in January 1886; Israel in September 1894.

9 *South Wales Daily News*, 12 November 1892; *Rhondda Leader*, 1 November 1902.

10 *Evening Express*, 30 June, 1 July 1905.

11 *Glamorgan Free Press*, 1 October 1898, 17 June 1899; *Pontypridd Chronicle*, 1 September 1899.

12 *Weekly Mail*, 9 March 1907.

13 *Daily Herald*, 19 August 1920.

14 His medal card shows that he landed in France on 30 August 1914. The National Archives, Kew, London: WO/372/7/98184-Medal Card of Floyd, William Mansell. See also his Red Cross service card, available online: https://vad.redcross.org.uk/Card?fname=william+&sname=floyd&id=76369 &first=true&last=true [Accessed: 2 December 2019]

15 Neither are identified by Billy Floyd in the diary, although it is possible that he worked at the No. 9 General Hospital which was situated in Nantes between September and November 1914, and from November 1914 in Rouen until it was taken over by American personnel in June 1917.

16 Imperial War Museum, London: Private Papers of W. M. Floyd. A copy is held at Pontypridd Museum, where it was consulted.

17 Although Israel Floyd, Billy's father, died in 1924.

18 Interview with Alun Hughes, February 2013. Notes in possession of the author.

19 *Daily Herald*, 1 September 1932; 13 March 1933.

20 *Daily Herald*, 26 March 1930.

21 *Daily Herald*, 1 May 1930.

22 *Cardiff Times*, 30 September 1932.

23 *Western Mail*, 3 March 1934.

24 Catherine Emily Bedford (1873-1941). Graduate of University College of South Wales and Monmouthshire, 1894. Trained in Greenwich and Newtown before being appointed as headmistress of Pontypridd Intermediate School for Girls in 1898. Remained in post until her retirement in 1935. She was replaced

by the school's senior mistress in foreign languages, Tonypandy-born Mary Jenkins. *South Wales Echo*, 18 November 1898; *Western Mail*, 29 January 1935.

25 *Western Mail*, 25 June 2010.

26 *Western Mail*, 1 September 1939.

27 *Western Mail*, 26 August 1939. Alongside Elaine were Iris Harris and Olwen Phillips.

28 The results of which were published in the *Western Mail*, 1 September 1939.

29 Grier served as principal of LMH between 1921 and 1945. Previously she had been Professor of Economics at Leeds University (1915-1919) and lecturer at Newnham College, Cambridge, where she had been a student.

30 Sylvia Harrop, 'Committee Women: Women on the Consultative Committee of the Board of Education, 1900-1944', in Joyce Goodman and Sylvia Harrop (eds.), *Women, Educational Policy Making and Administration in England: Authoritative Women since 1880* (London: Routledge, 2000), 167.

31 A.J. Chandler, 'The Re-Making of a Working Class: Migration from the South Wales coalfield to the new industry areas of the Midlands, c.1920-1940' (Unpublished PhD Thesis: University College of Cardiff, 1988), 177.

32 *The Magazine of the County Grammar School for Girls, Pontypridd, 1963* (Pontypridd, 1963), 8.

Chapter 2

1 Elaine Morgan, 'Lady Margaret Hall Potato Harvest', in Leigh Verrill-Rhys and Deirdre Beddoe (eds.), *Parachutes and Petticoats* (Dinas Powys: Honno, [1992] 2010 edn), 77-82.

2 Vera Brittain, *Women at Oxford* (New York: Macmillan, 1960), 198.

3 Bodleian Library, Ms.Eng.d.3364: Minute Book of the Oxford University Democratic Socialist Club, 1940-1942 (hereafter, OUDSC Minutes). The full background is given in an introduction to the minute book contained within. The club had first formed, in secret, on the 19 April 1940.

4 *Birmingham Daily Post*, 25 April 1940.

5 *Daily Herald*, 25 April 1940.

6 *Daily Herald*, 4 May 1940; *Western Morning News*, 4 May 1940.

7 OUDSC Minutes, Oxford terms are traditionally known as Michaelmas (October-December), Hilary January-March), and Trinity (May-July). In keeping with the sources, I have referred to this system rather than translate to a seasonal description of when each term was taking place.

8 Bodleian Library, Roy Jenkins Papers, MS Jenkins 495: Oxford University Democratic Socialist Club, Term Card for Trinity Term, 1940; Bjarne Braatov,

The New Sweden – A Vindication of Democracy (London: Thomas Nelson and Sons, 1939).

9 Jenkins Papers, Oxford University Democratic Socialist Club, Term Card for Hilary Term 1941; OUDSC Minutes, 2 March 1941.

10 OUDSC Minutes, 14 March 1941.

11 OUDSC Minutes, 14 March 1941.

12 OUDSC Minutes, 4 May 1941.

13 OUDSC Minutes, 15 June 1941.

14 OUDSC Minutes, 19 September 1941.

15 OUDSC Minutes, 24 November 1941.

16 OUDSC Minutes, 30 November 1941.

17 OUDSC Minutes, 23 November 1941.

18 OUDSC Minutes, 16 January 1942.

19 *The Scotsman*, 25 January 1941.

20 *The Cherwell*, 22 May 1941; a transcript of the talk can be found in George Orwell (Peter Davison, ed.), *A Patriot After All, 1940-1941* (London: Secker and Warburg, 1998), 501.

21 *The Independent,* 14 March 1993.

22 It is probable that Elaine also knew Kingsley Amis. He was certainly known to Drummond Allison – the two sang in the Labour Club choir together – although in Amis's own words 'never very well'. 'Letter from Kingsley Amis to Michael Sharp, 6 February 1974' in Zachary Leader (ed.), *The Letters of Kingsley Amis* (London: HarperCollins, 2000), 760. Michael Sharp was the editor of a collection of Allison's poems in 1978. Michael Sharp (ed.), *The Poems of Drummond Allison* (Reading: Whiteknights Press, 1978).

23 *The Guardian*, 18 August 2000.

24 Stephen Benson (ed), *The Collected Poems of Drummond Allison* (Reading, 1993), 16-18.

25 Michael Meyer and Sidney Keyes (eds), *Eight Oxford Poets* (Oxford, 1941); Ian Davie (ed.), *Oxford Poetry, 1942-1943* (Oxford, 1943). Further work appeared in Donald Bain and Antony Brown (eds.) *Z: Oxford and Cambridge Writing* (Cambridge, 1942). Allison's own collection, *The Yellow Night* (London: The Fortune Press) was published in 1944.

26 OUDSC Minutes, 11 March 1942.

27 *Western Mail*, 13 February 2009.

28 Morgan, *Knock 'Em Cold, Kid,* 51-52.

29 The relationship between the Oxford and extra mural education has been explored by Lawrence Goldman, *Dons and Workers* (Oxford: Clarendon Press,

1995). The treasurer of the Eastern District in this period was Lionel Elvin, fellow of Trinity Hall, Cambridge, and the son of Herbert Henry Elvin, general secretary of the National Union of Clerks and a leading figure in the Labour Party's sporting activities. Lionel was subsequently principal of Ruskin College, Oxford. Lionel Elvin, *Encounters with Education* (London, 1987).

30 Roger Fieldhouse, 'Thompson: The Adult Educator', in Fieldhouse and Richard Taylor (eds), *EP Thompson and English Radicalism* (Manchester: Manchester University Press, 2013); Tom Steele, *The Emergence of Cultural Studies* (London: Lawrence & Wishart, 1997).

31 Cited in Fred Inglis, *Raymond Williams* (London: Routledge, 1995), 113.

32 Cited in John Field, 'Survival, Growth and Retreat: The WEA in Wartime 1939-45', in Stephen Roberts (ed.), *A Ministry of Enthusiasm: Centenary Essays on the Workers' Educational Association* (London: Pluto, 2003) 133.

33 *Norfolk and Suffolk Journal and Diss Express*, 10 September, 24 September 1943; *Bury Free Press and Post*, 11 December 1943.

34 He was to graduate in 1940. *Western Mail*, 29 June 1940.

35 *Burnley Express*, 23 September 1944.

36 Morgan, *Knock Em Cold, Kid*, 67.

37 Although Dylan's first name, 'John', was clearly a nod to Morien's father; the choice of middle name (by which he was always known) was perhaps intended to recall the poet Dylan Thomas.

38 This was the impression conveyed by Dorothy Thompson to Dai Smith when the pair met to discuss the career of Raymond Williams and she contrasted the work of E.P. Thompson in Leeds with Williams in Norfolk and southern England.

39 *Burnley Express*, 3 October, 6 October 1945; 21 September 1946.

40 Note Elaine's ability to replace Morien at short notice. *Plebs* 39, no. 8 (August 19478), 140. "Mrs Elaine Morgan, MA, ably deputised for her husband who was unable to take the lectures due to illness. Wages, Prices and Profits and Women in Industry proved two popular subjects when handled by Mrs Morgan at the Hundsford School", *Plebs* 39, no.9 (September 1947), 160. 'the twenty-five students who enjoyed the excellent fare and first-class lectures of Bob Edwards and M.W.P. Morgan voted the event a great success. Bill Rathbone presided. The wind howled all night in traditional manner but the ghost on the corridor was not less substantial than Comrade Myatt of Crewe.' On their Communist Party membership see, for instance, *Burnley Express*, 3 September 1947.

41 *Burnley Express*, 27 September 1947.

42 *Burnley Express*, 12 October, 2 November 1946.

43 *Nelson Leader*, 19 September 1947, 24 September 1948. The classes were held at Whitefield Secondary Modern School.

44 *Burnley Express*, 9 October 1946.

45 *Burnley Express*, 16 October 1946.

46 *Burnley Express*, 19 October 1946. Radiorelay's reply was published on 26 October 1946.

47 *Burnley Express*, 9 November 1946. Elaine's previous response was published on 2 November 1946.

48 *Burnley Express*, 23 November 1946.

49 *Burnley Express*, 2 April 1947.

50 *Burnley Express*, 21 November, 8 December 1945; 11 June, 14 June, 18 June, 5 July 1947.

51 *Burnley Express*, 13 September 1947.

52 *Burnley Express*, 12 January, 19 January, 23 January, 2 February, 14 December, 21 December 1946.

53 Bailey, *Can Any Mother Help Me*, xxiii.

54 As above.

Chapter 3

1 BBC WAC, RCONT 12, Elaine Morgan, 1950-1963: Letter from PAD (secretary to Gale Pedrick) to Elaine Morgan, 9 May 1950'.

2 BBC WAC, RCONT 12, Elaine Morgan, 1950-1963: Letter from Peter Dion Titheradge to Elaine Morgan, 17 May 1950'.

3 BBC WAC, RCONT 12, Elaine Morgan, 1950-1963: Letter from Peter Dion Titheradge to Mai Jones, 17 May 1950'.

4 *Pontypridd Observer*, 28 October 1950.

5 BBC WAC, Microfilm Scripts, Woman's Hour: 26 October 1950.

6 BBC WAC, RCONT 12, Elaine Morgan, 1950-1963: Contributor Fee Memorandum, 3 November 1950.

7 *Radio Times*, 20 April 1951; 14 December 1951.

8 *Radio Times*, 7 March 1952.

9 *The Observer*, 28 December 1952. It also won her an accolade from Aberdare Chamber of Commerce. *Merthyr Express*, 17 January 1953.

10 *New Statesman and Nation*, 6 January 1951.

11 BBC WAC, WA8/382/1, Welsh Region Radio Talks, Elaine Morgan, 1950-1967: Letter from Aled Vaughan to Elaine Morgan, 18 June 1954.

12 BBC WAC, WA8/382/1, Letter from Aled Vaughan to Elaine Morgan, 27 July

1954; *Radio Times*, 6 August 1954.

13 BBC WAC, WA8/382/1, Letter from Nan Davies to Head of Welsh Programmes, A. Watkin Jones, 21 June 1954.

14 BBC WAC, WA8/328/1, Letter from A. Watkin Jones to Nan Davies, 22 June 1954.

15 *Western Mail*, 6 August 1954.

16 Elaine Morgan, 'The Welsh Schools', *The Highway* 45 (October 1953), 2-5.

17 Elaine Morgan, 'Five Day Week', *My Weekly*, 21 September 1953.

18 *New Statesman and Nation*, 13 February 1954.

19 *New Statesman and Nation*, 9 June 1951.

20 *New Statesman and Nation*, 9 February 1952.

21 *New Statesman and Nation*, 23 October 1954.

22 Jenna Bailey, Can Any Mother Help Me? (London: Faber & Faber, 2007); Elaine Morgan's original letters are held at University of Sussex Special Collections, The Keep, Brighton, Rose Hacker Papers, SxMOA24/1/3: 'Angharad'.

23 *Radio Times*, 18 March 1955.

24 *Western Mail*, 29 June 1956, 11 July 1956.

25 *Liverpool Echo*, 21 March 1955.

26 *The Stage*, 24 March 1955.

27 BBC WAC, T48/437/5, TV Scriptwriters, Elaine Morgan, File 1: Television Drama Report on The Golden World by Elaine Morgan, by Joyce O'Donovan, 7 January 1954.

28 *Western Mail*, 4 October 1955, 7 February 1956; *Daily Telegraph*, 8 February 1956; *Algemeen Handelsblad*, 11 January 1956; *De Telegraaf*, 10 January 1956.

29 BBC WAC, T48/437/5, Memoradum from BBC Play Library to Script Unit on The Tamer Tamed by Elaine Morgan, 6 April 1956.

30 BBC WAC, T48/437/5: Memorandum from Helena Wood to Script Editor, Drama (Sound) on The Tamer Tamed by Elaine Morgan, 16 May 1956.

31 *Western Mail*, 28 September 1955; *Writers and Artists Year Book, 1957* (London: Adam and Charles Black, 1957), 273.

32 *Daily Mail*, 9 December 1955.

33 *Daily Telegraph*, 9 December 1955.

34 *Western Mail*, 13 February 1956.

35 BBC WAC, T48/437/1, Drama Writer's File, Elaine Morgan, 1955-1957: Memorandum from Donald Wilson to Michael Barry, 28 September 1955.

36 BBC WAC, T48/437/1, Memorandum from Mary Adams to Michael Barry, 14 December 1955.

37 BBC WAC, T48/437/1, Letter from Donald Wilson to Elaine Morgan, 19

March 1956.

38 *The People*, 27 January 1957.

39 *Western Mail*, 5 February 1957.

40 BBC WAC,T48/437/l, Letter from Donald Wilson to Michael Barry, 29 March 1956.

41 *Liverpool Echo*, 11 July 1956.

42 *Western Mail*, 11 July 1956.

43 BBC WAC, T48/437/l, Letter from Donald Wilson to Elaine Morgan, 19 March 1956.

44 R.J.C.Atkinson, *Stonehenge* (London: Hamish Hamilton, 1956).Atkinson was appointed as the first professor of archaeology at Cardiff in 1958.

45 BBC WAC,T48/437/l, Letter from Elaine Morgan to Donald Wilson, undated but March 1956.

46 BBC WAC,T48/437/l, Letter to Elaine Morgan from Donald Wilson, 6 September 1956.

47 BBC WAC,T48/437/1, Letter from Alan Bromly to Assistant Head of Drama, Television, 2 November 1956. Broadcast had initially been pencilled for 17 January 1957.

48 *Daily Mirror*, 27 May 1957; *Daily Herald*, 27 May 1957; *The Stage*, 30 May 1957.

49 *Kensington Post*, 4 January 1957.The Kensington-Paddington Family Service Unit was located at the time at 36 Colville Terrace and had been established, albeit in Westbourne Grove, in 1948. *Kensington Post*, 12 August 1955.

50 *Shields Daily News*, 3 January 1957.

51 *Western Mail*, 7 January 1957.

52 BBC WAC,T48/437/l, Letter from John Elliot to Elaine Morgan, 3 December 1956.

53 BBC WAC,T48/437/l, Letter from Elaine Morgan to John Elliot, 4 June 1956.

54 BBC WAC,T48/437/l, Letter from Elaine Morgan to John Elliot, 6 July 1956.

55 A.F. Philip, *Family Failure* (London: Faber and Faber, 1963).The book carried a foreword by Sir John Wolfenden.

56 BBC WAC,T48/437/l, Letter and treatment for FSU from Elaine Morgan, 5 September 1956.

57 BBC WAC,T48/437/l, Letter from Elaine Morgan to John Elliot, undated but October 1956.

58 BBC WAC,T48/437/l, Letter from Elaine Morgan to John Elliot, undated by January 1957.

59 The Tryweryn drama-documentary, with its borrowed Emlyn Williams title

'The Last Days of Dowlyn', was eventually shelved. Letter from John Elliot to Elaine Morgan, 8 August 1957.

60 *Western Mail*, 31 March 1958.

61 *Western Mail*, 16 July 1956.

62 *Western Mail*, 4 April 1956.

63 *Radio Times*, 12 October 1972.

64 Janet Thumim, *Inventing Television Culture: Men, Women, and the Box* (Oxford: Oxford University Press, 2004), 51.

65 Suzanne Franks, 'Attitudes to Women in the BBC in the 1970s – Not So Much a Glass Ceiling as One of Reinforced Concrete', *Westminster Papers in Communication and Culture* 8, no. 3 (2011), 123.

66 Cited in Franks, 'Attitudes', 128-9.

67 Morgan, 'Women's Contribution', 212.

68 Elaine Aston, 'Foreword', in Shelagh Delaney, *A Taste of Honey* (London: Methuen, 2008 edn.), v; Selina Todd, *Tastes of Honey: The Making of Shelagh Delaney and a Cultural Revolution* (London: Vintage, 2019).

69 *Western Mail*, 12 May 1958.

70 A point underlined by the BBC's *Television New Writing* series launched in September 1960, which included plays by John Osborne and Elaine.

71 BBC WAC, Scripts Library Microfilm, *Any Questions*, 3 January 1964.

72 South Wales District of the Workers' Educational Association, *Forty Eighth Annual Report* (Cardiff: WEA, 1955), 25; South Wales District of the Workers' Educational Association, *Fiftieth Annual Report* (Cardiff: WEA, 1957), 34-35; South Wales District of the Workers' Educational Association, *Fifty First Annual Report* (Cardiff: WEA, 1958), 28.

73 The tablets were manufactured by Vitamins Ltd and first appeared in Britain in 1935. *The Chemist and Druggist*, 5 October 1935.

74 BBC WAC, T48/437 /l, Letter from Elaine Morgan to Donald Wilson, undated but October 1957.

75 Rose Hacker was also a notable writer on sex education in the 1950s and 1960s. Her *Telling the Teenagers: A Guide to Parents, Teachers and Youth Leaders* (London: Andre Deutsch, 1957) was widely read and revised and reprinted a number of times in the 1960s under the title *The Opposite Sex*. Rose Hacker, *Abraham's Daughter: The Autobiography of Rose Hacker* (London: Deptford Forum Publishing, 1996) tells her story.

76 *Western Mail*, 20 October 1958.

77 Modern Records Centre, Warwick, Victor Gollancz Papers, MSS.157/3/ND/1 – Letters regarding Aberdare and Mountain Ash Ban the Bomb Committee,

August 1958; McMaster University Special Collections, Canada, Bertrand Russell Papers: 1.44 RAl 630, Letter from W. D. Richards, Secretary, Aberdare and Mountain Ash Ban-the-Bomb Committee for Nuclear Disarmament to Bertrand Russell, 22 August 1958; 11.15 RAl 750, Letter from Bertrand Russell to W. D. Richards, 22 August 1958; 1.45 RAl 630 Letter from Gareth Edwards, Secretary of Aberdare CND to Bertrand Russell, 16 September 1961.

78 *Western Mail,* 25 August, 15 September 1958.

79 Kathleen Burk, *Troublemaker: The Life and History of A.J.P. Taylor* (New Haven: Yale University Press, 2000), 212-217.

80 Hilda Price, 'A Political Life', in Deirdre Beddoe (ed.), *Changing Times: Welsh Women Writing on the 1950s and 1960s* (Dinas Powys: Honno), 275-6; see also the back flap of *Falling Apart* (1976).

81 *Daily Telegraph,* 1 April 1963. When it arrived in Liverpool for a highly successful run in the autumn of 1964, the defence lawyer was played by John Savident.

82 *Coventry Evening Telegraph,* 25 May 1963.

83 *Daily Express,* 17 May 1965.

84 *The Stage,* 3 March 1960.

85 *Liverpool Echo,* 17 May 1960

Chapter 4

1 *Daily Mail,* 23 January 1957, 21 March 1957.

2 BBC WAC, T48/437/l, Letter from Donald Wilson to Elaine Morgan, 21 February 1957.

3 BBC WAC, T48/437/l, Letter from Elaine Morgan to Donald Wilson, undated but July 1957.

4 BBC WAC, T48/437/l, Letter from Elaine Morgan to Donald Wilson, undated but February 1958.

5 BBC WAC, T48/437/l, Letter from Donald Wilson to Elaine Morgan, 3 February 1958.

6 BBC WAC, T48/437/l, Letter from Elaine Morgan to John Elliot, 18 March 1958.

7 BBC WAC, T48/437/l, Letter from Elaine Morgan to Donald Wilson, undated but June 1958.

8 BBC WAC, T48/437/l, Treatment for 'They Can't Take It From You', undated but November 1958.

9 BBC WAC, T48/437/l, Letter from Donald Wilson to Elaine Morgan, 9 December 1958.

10 BBC WAC, T48/437/l, Letter from Elaine Morgan to Donald Wilson, undated but December 1958. Elaine's reference, here, was to Dennis Potter's involvement in Christopher Mayhew's 1958 series *Does Class Matter?* Mayhew, at the time, was Labour MP for Woolwich East, the seat formerly held by Ernest Bevin. Potter had gone up to New College, Oxford, in 1956 following National Service, and was chair of the Labour Club as well as editor of the literary magazine *Isis*.

11 BBC WAC, T48/437/l, Letter from Elaine Morgan to Donald Wilson, undated but December 1958.

12 BBC WAC, T48/437/l, Letter from Donald Wilson to Elaine Morgan, 30 January 1959.

13 BBC WAC, T48/437/2, Letter from Donald Wilson to Elaine Morgan, 7 March 1960.

14 BBC WAC, T48/437/l, Letter from Betty Willingale to Elaine Morgan, 8 May 1959. Wilson's comments are added in red pencil.

15 BBC WAC, T48/437/l, Letter from Donald Wilson to Elaine Morgan, 15 May 1959.

16 BBC WAC, T48/437/l, Letter from Donald Wilson to Elaine Morgan, 25 June 1959.

17 BBC WAC, T48/437/2, Letter from Elaine Morgan to Donald Wilson, 16 February 1960.

18 BBC WAC, T48/437/2, Letter from Elaine Morgan to Donald Wilson, 25 May 1960.

19 Berry, *Wales and the Cinema,* 360.

20 *Liverpool Echo,* 21 June 1960.

21 *Birmingham Daily Post,* 29 June 1960.

22 *The Stage,* 10 December 1964, 15 April 1965, 2 September 1965.

23 *Liverpool Echo,* 3 July 1965.

24 *The Stage,* 29 July 1965.

25 BBC WAC, RCONT 1, Elaine Morgan Copyright File 1, 1959-1962, Invoice from John Johnson, Author's Agent, to BBC Copyright Department, 31 July 1959.

26 BBC WAC, RCONT 1, Elaine Morgan, Letter from BBC Copyright Department to John Johnson, 7 January 1958.

27 BBC WAC, RCONT 1, Elaine Morgan, Letter from Donald Wilson to Head of Script Department, 20 October 1960.

28 *The Times,* 5 August 2003.

29 As above.

30 Another on his list was Elaine's fellow Pontypriddian, Alun Richards.

31 Not to be confused with the programme of the same name, presented by Richard Crossman and produced by Elwyn Jones, which was broadcast on BBC One in 1973.

32 Letter from Donald Wilson to David Whitaker, 20 July 1962, in BBC WAC, T48/437/2. Whitaker went on to be the primary story editor for *Doctor Who* from its inception in 1963 until 1964.

33 George Ewart Evans, *The Voices of the Children* (Cardigan: Parthian, 2008), x. The book was first published in 1947.

34 Letter from Harry Green to Elaine Morgan, 12 October 1962 in BBC WAC, T48/437/2.

35 *The Stage*, 21 February 1963.

36 Letter from Harry Green to Elaine Morgan, 4 January 1963 in BBC WAC, T48/437/2.

37 *The Stage*, 28 November 1963.

38 *Belfast Telegraph*, 9 November 1963.

39 *Coventry Evening Telegraph*, 1 October 1963.

40 *The Stage*, 5 May 1960.

41 *The Stage*, 12 May 1960.

42 Letter from Elaine Morgan to Donald Wilson, 30 May 1963 in BBC WAC, T48/437/2.

43 *The Stage*, 2 July 1964.

44 Letter from Elaine Morgan to Sydney Newman, 13 May 1966 in BBC WAC, T48/437/2.

45 Letter from Verity Lambert to Andrew Osborn, 2 August 1967 in BBC WAC, T48/437/2.

46 Letter from Anthony Read to Andrew Osborn, 3 August 1967 in BBC WAC, T48/437/2.

47 Elaine's relationship with ITV had much to do with her friendship with Ted Willis. Willis got to know Elaine through the Screen Writer's Guild, the writer's trade union, of which Willis was chair from its creation in 1958 until he stepped down in 1964. In his youth, Willis had been active in the Labour Party and the Communist Party and wrote for the *Daily Worker* as its drama critic. Elaine's first ITV script was broadcast as part of *Inside Story* in 1960. *The Stage*, 14 January 1960. The series was produced by Sydney Newman. Elaine's episode was 'The Conspiracy' broadcast on 13 March 1960.

48 The series suffered significantly from the policy of wiping telerecordings and only one episode has survived.

49 *The Stage*, 12 September 1968.

50 *The Stage* 18 September 1969.

51 *Daily Telegraph*, 29 December 2015; *The Guardian*, 18 July 2017.

Chapter 5

1 Elaine Morgan, 'Introduction' in F. Tennyson Jesse, *A Pin to see the Peepshow* (London: Virago, 1979). The transcript of the trial was almost certainly Filson Young (ed), *Trial of Frederick Bywaters and Edith Thompson* (Edinburgh: William Hodge & Co, 1923), which was part of the Notable British Trials series.

2 *The Stage*, 2 May, 16 May 1974. The other nominees were Geoffrey Lancashire for 'Shabby Tiger' on ITV, and Hugh Whitemore for 'The Adventures of Don Quixote' on the BBC.

3 Clive James, 'Women's Lab', *The Observer*, 28 August, 1977.

4 Clive James, 'I am a tropical fish', *The Observer*, 16 November 1980.

5 Sian Phillips interviewed in *Great Welsh Writers: Elaine Morgan* (BBC 1 Wales, 2 March 2013).

6 *Birmingham Daily Post*, 26 June 1974.

7 *Liverpool Echo*, 10 December 1974.

8 *The Stage*, 18 September, 2 October 1975; *Liverpool Echo*, 17 March 1975.

9 *Radio Times*, 18 August 1977.

10 Mark Bostridge, *Vera Brittain and the First World War: The Story of Testament of Youth* (London: Bloomsbury, 2014), 161. I have followed his description of Elaine's role in what follows.

11 *Western Mail*, 30 April 2010.

12 Clive James, 'Mother of Shirley Williams', *The Observer*, 11 November 1979.

13 *The Stage*, 5 June 1980.

14 Robert Reid, *Marie Curie* (London: Collins, 1974).

15 *The Stage*, 26 May 1977.

16 The film was ostensibly based on the 1936 biography by Eve Curie, the younger daughter of Marie and Pierre.

17 *Reading Evening Post*, 16 August 1977.

18 *Aberdeen Press and Journal*, 20 August 1977.

19 *The Stage*, 23 February, 23 March 1978.

20 Sian Phillips won a BAFTA for her portrayal of Beth Morgan. Others in the company included familiar faces such as Nerys Hughes (of the *Liver Birds*), Ray Smith (then most famous as Detective Inspector Percy Firbank of *Public Eye*), and Gareth Hughes, who would later star as the eponymous hero of the science fiction series *Blake's 7*.

21 *The Stage*, 8 January 1976.
22 Richard Llewellyn, *Up Into the Singing Mountain* (London: Michael Joseph, 1960); Richard Llewellyn, *Down Where the Moon is Small* (London: Michael Joseph, 1966).
23 *Belfast Telegraph*, 26 April 1977.
24 *Daily Mirror*, 3 January 1976.
25 Commissioning Brief for How Green Was My Valley, 22 April 1975, in BBC WAC, T48/437/5.
26 *The Stage*, 16 June 1977.
27 *The Stage*, 21 August 1975.
28 *Daily Mirror*, 20 March 1971.
29 Deirdre Beddoe, 'Easter Conference, 1983', *Llafur* 4, no. 1 (1984), 100; Angela V. John, 'Llafur Easter School, 8-10 April 1983', *History Workshop Journal* 16, no. 1 (Autumn 1983), 176; British Library Sound Archive, C1420/23, 'Sisterhood and After: The Women's Liberation Oral History Project: Deirdre Beddoe'. Available Online: https://www.bl.uk/collection-items/deirdre-beddoe organising-the-first-welsh-womens-history-conference
30 *Independent*, 26 July 1997; Western Mail, 11 February 2011.
31 The original source was George Ewart Evans's short story, *Possessions*, which had first been published in *Chamber's Journal* in 1952 – although was probably more widely known (and certainly more accessible) from Gwyn Jones's *Welsh Short Stories* collection of 1956. George Ewart Evans, 'Possessions', *Chamber's Journal* July 1952, 435-440; George Ewart Evans, 'Possessions', in Gwyn Jones (ed), *Welsh Short Stories* (London: Oxford University Press, 1956). Gareth Williams has noted that this is one of George Ewart Evans's most anthologised short stories. See his: *George Ewart Evans* (Cardiff: University of Wales Press, 1991), 5.
32 Correspondence between the two is preserved at the National Library of Wales and at the South Wales Miners' Library.
33 Emrys Hughes married Keir Hardie's daughter, Nan, in 1924 and wrote a biography of his father in law in 1956.
34 *The Stage*, 2 April 1964, 2 July 1964; *Radio Times*, 18 June 1964.
35 *Radio Times*, 28 February 1981, 11 April 1981, 16 May 1981. The series was novelised by David Benedictus as *Lloyd George: The Novel* in 1981.
36 The coincidence was noted at the time by the television critic for the *Reading Evening Post*, 8 January 1982.
37 *Newcastle Evening Chronicle*, 5 February 1982.
38 Elaine Morgan, 'Dashing Renaissance Polymath or Mild-Mannered Spinster?',

The Listener, 11 February 1982.

39 *The Stage*, 20 February 1986.

40 Betka Zamoyska, *The Burston Rebellion* (London: Ariel Books, 1985)

41 Tom Higdon wrote his own account of the strike. T.G. Higdon, *The Burston Rebellion* (Manchester: The National Labour Press, 1917). Based on her middle name Catherine, Annie was often known as Kitty.

42 John Naughton, 'Television', *The Listener*, 28 February 1985.

43 John Naughton, 'Television', *The Listener*, 15 January 1987.

44 *The Stage*, 10 December 1992, 29 April 1993,

45 *Western Mail*, 2 July 1957, 7 November 1959.

46 South Wales Miners' Library, *Newsletter* 1 (May 1991), 2.

47 *Independent*, 12 March 1994.

48 Desmond Morris, *The Naked Ape: A Zoologist's Study of the Human Animal* (London: Jonathan Cape, 1967).

Chapter 6

1 Including Croatian, Danish, Dutch, Finnish, French, German, Greek, Italian, Japanese, Norwegian, Swedish and Spanish; Beddoe, *Out of the Shadows*, 160.

2 Morgan, *The Descent of Woman*, 10-11.

3 *Kensington Post*, 27 October 1972.

4 Columbia University, New York, Rare Book and Manuscript Library: Stein & Day Publisher Records, Box 18-Descent of Woman, 1972.

5 *Western Mail*, 17 February 1972. The sum reflected the $100,000 paid for the paperback rights by Bantam Press, translation rights, and serialisation fees for *The Observer* in the UK and *McCall's* magazine in the United States.

6 'Behavior: A Wet Scenario', *Time*, 19 June 1972.

7 *Daily Express*, 30 June 1972; *The Observer*, 17 September, 24 September, 1 October 1972.

8 *Daily Mirror*, 19 October 1972. The documentary coincidence with the UK release of *Descent of Woman* on 5 October 1972.

9 *Sunday Telegraph*, 27 February 1972. The book was published in the United States on 31 May 1972. *Publisher's Weekly* 201 (1972), 217.

10 *The Guardian*, 10 May 1972.

11 Stein & Day Records, Box 18, Folder 1: 'Letter from Elaine Morgan to Ernest Hecht, Souvenir Press, 21 November 1971'; 'Letter from Sol Stein to Ernest Hecht, 29 November 1971'.

12 Jordan Bonfante, 'The Naked Ape is all wet, says a Liberated Lady', *Life*, 21 July 1972; *New York Times*, 8 May 1972.

13 *Toronto Star*, 12 May 1972.

14 *New York Times*, 8 May 1972.

15 Although this was the only occasion it did so. Stein & Day Records, Box 18, Folder 1, 'Memo on DESCENT OF WOMAN – Morgan, 9 August 1972'.

16 *New York Times*, Sunday Book Review, 25 June 1972.

17 Marian Engel, 'She makes mincemeat of the Tarzan and Flintstone set', *Globe and Mail*, 9 September 1972. The book was published by J. M. Dent in Canada.

18 *The Canberra Times*, 17 March 1973. Both Australia and New Zealand received imports of the Souvenir Press edition from London.

19 Victoria Brittain, 'The Origin of Water Babies?', *The Times*, 4 October 1972.

20 Mary Stott, 'Is This What The Men Forgot?', *Daily Mail*, 5 October 1972.

21 University of Toronto, Department of Extension, *Continuing Education Programme Calendar, 1973-4* (Toronto: University of Toronto, 1973), 15. The theme is more widely considered in Erika Lorraine Milam, *Creatures of Cain: The Hunt for Human Nature in Cold War America* (Princeton: Princeton University Press, 2019), ch. 9.

22 *The Guardian*, 12 January 2007.

23 Dale Spender, Men's *Studies Modified: The Impact of Feminism on the Academic Disciplines* (Oxford: Pergamon, 1981) and *For the Record: The Making and Meaning of Feminist Knowledge* (London: The Women's Press, 1985).

24 Pat Barr, *The Framing of the Female* (London: Kestrel Books, 1978).

25 'Me Jane, You Tarzan – Elaine Morgan interviewed by Lois Hansen and Julia Curtis, KPFA Radio, 18 May 1972'. Recording available online: https://archive.org/details/pacifica_radio_archives-BC0952 [accessed 28 April 2019]

26 Carole Dix, 'Review of *Descent of Woman* by Elaine Morgan', *Spare Rib* 6 (December 1972), 30.

27 Michelene Wandor, 'Reviews', *Spare Rib* 9 (March 1973), 28.

28 *Belfast Telegraph*, 10 February 1973.

29 Jilly Boyce Kay, 'Speaking Bitterness: Second-Wave Feminism, Televison Talk, and the Case of *No Man's Land* (1973', *Feminist Media Histories* 1, no. 2 (2015), 64-89.

30 A copy of the programme is held at the British Film Institute Archive in London. An overview of the episode is provided here: http://www.bfi.org.uk/films-tv-people/4ce2b8c4ea2b2 [accessed: 27 April 2019] 31 Elaine Morgan, 'In Defense of Virgins', *New York Times*, 25 November 1977. The column had been broadcast on BBC Radio 4 in July 1977. *Birmingham Daily Post*, 20 July 1977.

32 *New York Times*, 14 December 1977.

33 Elaine Morgan, Women and Society (London: BBC, 1975).

34 Peter Lewis, 'The decline and fall of the Super Cities', *Daily Mail*, 21 October 1976.

35 *Daily Telegraph*, 20 October 1976.

36 Kohr was likewise a key influence on Plaid Cymru during his time living in Aberystwyth, becoming a mentor to Gwynfor Evans. His early pamphlet, *An Austrian Looks at Welsh Nationalism* (Aberystwyth: Plaid Cymru, 1959) signalled his involvement with the Welsh nationalists. Several Plaid Cymru activists, including Phil Williams and Gwynfor Evans, also wrote for *Resurgence*.

37 Morgan, *Falling Apart*, 262.

38 *Coventry Evening Telegraph*, 14 November 1969.

39 For her book reviews: *Resurgence* 9, no. 1 (March-April 1978), 36-43; *Resurgence* 9, no. 3 (September-October 1978), 29-39;

40 Leopold Kohr, 'Falling Apart', *Resurgence* 7, no. 6 Qanuary-February 1977), 26; Elaine Morgan, 'Revitalising the City 2: The Urban Octopus', *The New Ecologist* 3 (May/June 1978), 86-87.

41 Gerard Morgan-Grenville established the Centre for Alternative Technology near Machynlleth in 1973.

42 Elaine Morgan, *The Aquatic Ape: A Theory of Human Evolution* (London: Souvenir Press, 1982); *The* Bookseller, 13 February 1982, 185. The book appeared in America in December: *Publisher's Weekly* 222 (1982), 63.

43 The conference proceedings were published by Souvenir Press in 1991. Machteld Roede et al (eds), *The Aquatic Ape: Fact or Fiction?* (London: Souvenir Press, 1991). Elaine's contribution was 'What a New Theory is Needed', 9-22.

44 The impact of these works of the 1990s on evolutionary biology is considered in Erika Lorraine Milam, 'Debunking the Tarzanists: Elaine Morgan and the Aquatic Ape Theory' in Oren Harman and Michael Dietrich (eds.), *Outsider Scientists: Routes to Innovation in Biology* (Chicago: University of Chicago Press, 2013).

45 Richard Dawkins, *Brief Candle in the Dark: My Life in Science* (London: Bantam Press, 2015). Dawkins wrote supportively of Elaine's work on the aquatic ape theory, for a period. Richard Dawkins, 'Review of: Johnathan Kingdom, *Self-Made Man and His Undoing*', *Times Literary Supplement*, 26 March 1993.

46 *The Guardian*, 26 August 1992.

Chapter 7

1 *Western Mail*, 31 January 2003.
2 *Western Mail*, 7 February 2003.
3 *Western Mail*, 14 February 2003.
4 *Western Mail*, 20 February 2004.
5 *Western Mail*, 14 March 2004.
6 *Western Mail*, 17 December 2004.
7 *Western Mail*, 1 April 2005.
8 *Western Mail*, 20 April 2007.
9 *Western Mail*, 13 May 2005.
10 *Western Mail*, 29 July 2005.
11 *Western Mail*, 25 November 2005.
12 *Western Mail*, 15 September 2006.
13 *Western Mail*, 17 August 2007.
14 *Western Mail*, 3 July 2009.
15 *Western Mail*, 16 April 2010.
16 *Western Mail*, 16 September 2011.
17 *Western Mail*, 22 July 2011.
18 *Western Mail*, 19 February 2010.
19 *Western Mail*, 18 March 2011.
20 *Western Mail*, 25 May 2012.
21 *Western Mail*, 24 August 2012.
22 *Western Mail*, 8 June 2012.
23 *Western Mail*, 24 August, 21 September 2012, 4 January 2013.
24 *Western Mail*, 4 April 2013.
25 *Western Mail*, 4 March 2013.
26 Algis V. Kuliukas and Elaine Morgan, 'Aquatic Scenarios in the Thinking on Human Evolution: What are they and How do they Compare?', in Mario Vaneechoutte, Algis Kuliukas and Marc Verhaegen (eds.), *Was Man More Aquatic in the Past? Fifty Years After Alister Hardy Waterside Hypotheses of Human Evolution* (Amsterdam: Bentham, 2011), 106-119.
27 *Western Mail*, 13 July 2013.
28 *Western Mail*, 25 July 2013.
29 *Western Mail*, 26 July 2013.

ACKNOWLEDGEMENTS

Growing up near Pontypridd, I have always been aware of Elaine Morgan, although it was Morien Morgan who first came into my consciousness as a young man – he was from Ynysybwl, like me, and attended Trerobart Primary School and Pontypridd Intermediate School for Boys. By the time I got to the latter it was called Coedylan Comprehensive School, but the classrooms, the corridors and the school buildings were nearly all the same. Some of my school teachers must have known him, too, although I never had reason to ask them, at least not then. For a short period, in the last year or two of her life, I corresponded with Elaine thinking that I might write something about Morien, the international brigader, and his father, John E. Morgan, the miners' leader. She encouraged me to do so and to make sure I could never forget, wrote about our exchange in the Pensioner. Anyone who ever had occasion to write to, or visit, Aberffrwd Road in Mountain Ash can attest to the remarkable character of the encounter. Slowly, but surely, I realised that to write about Morien and Johnny (as she called him), I also needed to write about Elaine herself.

In the nearly ten years since that initial idea of writing biographically about Elaine, Morien, and John E Morgan, was first pondered, the centenary of Elaine's birth in Pontypridd in 1920 has come into view. Several years ago, on the way home from the South Wales Miners' Library, Alun Burge suggested writing a dual study of Elaine and the novelist Gwyn Thomas. On the surface, the two individuals shared a very similar trajectory – from the valleys to Oxford and back again – but as adults they came to reflect the two sides of the South Walian personality. Gwyn, the pre-eminent writer of and about American Wales, with his operatic tonality and global aspiration, and capacity to understand 'the joke'. Elaine, the writer who sought to bridge the divide between valleys and the rest of Wales through language, environmentalism, and the voices of women. This duality continues to resonate in the Wales of today.

As always, my writing has been supported by the local studies libraries, university archives, and county archives of South Wales. I am grateful to libraries in Pontypridd, Aberdare, and Cathays; to Pontypridd Museum; to the Glamorgan Archives and the Richard Burton Archives at Swansea University; to the South Wales Miners' Library; to the Bodleian Library; to the British Library; to the National Library of Wales; and to the BBC's Written Archive Centre in Reading (especially to Katy Ackers and Lou North, the archivists who assisted me). Remote assistance has been provided by Columbia University in New York City, the Norfolk Record Office, the Keep (Sussex Archives), Seven Stories: The National Centre for Children's Books, Samuel French Ltd, the Pacifica Radio Archives, the Australian Broadcasting Corporation, and the Canadian Broadcasting Corporation. Elements of this book were first presented as classes in Merthyr Tydfil and Oakdale, and to a meeting of the Gelligaer Historical Society at Llancaiach Fawr. I am especially grateful to all those present on those occasions for sharing their memories with me. Particular thanks are due to Ann Wilson, Alun Williams, Hywel Davies, Carolyn Jacob, Mary and Wilf Owen, Maria Williams, and Ceinwen Statter.

This book has, as ever, benefitted enormously from the guidance and support of Dai Smith, Hywel Francis, and Carolyn Hitt – who kindly agreed to provide the foreword and readily shared my view that Elaine deserved a full-length scholarly biography to establish her major contribution to Welsh public life. This view was willingly shared by Sarah Morse and Mick Felton, who embraced the book and have given it a marvellous welcome on the Seren list. Finally, this book is dedicated to my niece, Kate, in the hope that she may take inspiration from Elaine Morgan's life and realise her own dreams, whatever they may be.

NOTES ON SOURCES

Elaine Morgan did not leave behind a significant literary archive, except for the deposit of many – though by no means all – of her scripts to Swansea University. The absence of such an archive has been mitigated somewhat by examination of source material from several institutions in Britain and the United States. Of these, the BBC Written Archives Centre in Reading, the British Film Institute Archive in London, the Keep (Sussex Archives) in Brighton, the Bodleian Library in Oxford, and Columbia University's Special Collections in New York City, proved to be the most substantial. Smaller collections have been found at the Glamorgan Archives in Cardiff; the college archives at Lady Margaret Hall, Oxford; the National Library of Wales in Aberystwyth; the archives at the National Space Centre; Somerville College, Oxford; the University of Reading; the Norfolk Archives; the Lancashire Archives; the Labour History Archive and Study Centre in Manchester; the British Library; and the Harry Ransom Center at the University of Texas. Precise archival references, for those readers who may require them, can be found in the endnotes.

As a writer and broadcaster, Elaine was prolific, producing anything from poems to multi-part television programmes. Her broadcasting career, alone, spanned four decades and resulted in scores of scripts (primarily for the BBC). No less indicative of this remarkable output were the more than fifty successful entries to the *New Statesman* writing competitions in the early 1950s, as well as articles for student publications at Oxford, such as the *Oxford Socialist*, which no longer appear to be extant. The following list of her publications and broadcasts is, therefore, necessarily selective. I have grouped items by topic or theme, in what follows, and then arranged each of those segments chronologically to give an overall sense of the changing nature of Elaine's career.

PART 1: WRITING

A: BOOKS IN ORDER OF PUBLICATION

The Descent of Woman (London: Souvenir Press, 1972)

Women and Society (London: BBC, 1975)

Falling Apart: The Rise and Decline of Urban Civilization (London: Souvenir Press, 1976)

The Aquatic Ape: A Theory of Human Evolution (London: Souvenir Press, 1982)

The Descent of Woman (London: Souvenir Press, 1985 revised edition)

The Scars of Evolution (London: Souvenir Press, 1990)

The Descent of the Child: Human Evolution from a New Perspective (London: Souvenir Press, 1994)

The Aquatic Ape Hypothesis (London: Souvenir Press, 1997)

Pinker's List (Leeds: Eildon Press, 2005)

The Naked Darwinist (Leeds: Eildon Press, 2008)

Knock 'Em Cold, Kid (Kibworth Beauchamp: Matador, 2012)

B: PLAYS IN ORDER OF PUBLICATION

The Waiting Room: A Play for Women in One Act (London: Samuel French, 1958)

Rest You Merry: A Christmas Play in Two Acts (London: Samuel French, 1959)

'You're a Long Time Dead', in Michael Barry (ed.), *The Television Playwright* (London: Michael Joseph, 1960)

The Solider and the Woman: A Play in One Act (London: Samuel French, 1961)

Licence to Murder: A Play in Two Acts (London: Samuel French, 1963)

A Chance to Shine: A Play in One Act (London: Samuel French, 1964)

Love from Liz (London: Samuel French, 1967)

C: UNCOLLECTED SHORT STORIES, ESSAYS, AND JUVENILIA

'Kitty in Blunderland', *Weekly Mail* and *Cardiff Times*, 1 October 1932

'Emblematic of the Nation', *Western Mail*, 3 March 1934

'Five Day Week', *My Weekly*, 21 September 1953

'The Aquatic Hypothesis', *New Scientist* 102 (12 April 1984), 11-13.

'Sweaty Old Man and the Sea', *New Scientist* 105 (21 March 1985), 27-28.

'In the Beginning was the Water', *New Scientist* 109 (6 March 1986), 13-15.

'Lucy's Child', *New Scientist* 112 (25 December 1986), 13-15.

'The Water Baby', *New Statesman* 5, no. 232 (12 December 1992), 29-30.

'Bipedalism', *Nutrition and Health* 9, no. 3 (1993), 193-203.

'Walking Hypothesis', *New Statesman* 7, no. 305 (3 June 1994), 37-38.

'Four Legs Good', *New Scientist* 195, no. 2615 (2007), 20.

'Who are the modern humans?', *New Scientist* 196, no. 2631 (2007), 57.

'Here Comes Everybody', *New Statesman* (24 July 2008), 45.

'You're So Special', *New Scientist* 198, no. 2661 (2008), 26.

'Orangutans and Us', *New Scientist* 201, no. 2698 (2009), 26-27.

'Female Prostate', *New Scientist* 203, no. 2715 (2009), 24.

'Why are we the naked ape?', *New Scientist* 203, no. 2726 (2009), 28-29.

'Kind Lies', *New Scientist* 207, no. 2768 (2010), 25.

'Was Man More Aquatic in the Past', *Nutrition and Health* 16, no. 1 (2002), 23-24.

'The Aquatic Ape Theory and the Origin of Speech', in Jan Wind, Edwin Pulleyblank and Eric de Grolier (eds.), *Studies in Language Origins* 1 (Philadelphia: Benjamins, 1989), 199-208.

'Olive', in Sian Rhiannon Williams and Carole White (eds), *Struggle or Starve: Women's Lives in the South Wales Valleys Between the Two World Wars* (Dinas Powys: Honno, 2002)

'The LMH Potato Harvest' in Leigh Verrill-Rhys and Deirdre Beddoe (eds), *Parachutes and Petticoats: Welsh Women Writing on the Second World War* (Dinas Powys: Honno, 1992).

'Living at the end of the world', in Deirdre Beddoe (ed.), *Changing Times: Welsh Women Writing on the 1950s and 1960s* (Dinas Powys: Honno, 2003).

'Women and the Future', in Robert Bundy (ed.), *Images of the Future: The Twenty First Century and Beyond* (Buffalo, NY: Prometheus Books, 1976), 143-151.

'Writing for Television: Women's Contribution', *Women's Studies International Quarterly* 2, no. 2 (1979), 209-213.

'Greatest Story Ever Told', *Radio Times* 13-19 January 1979, 77.

'Introduction', in Dorothy Edwards, *Winter Sonata* (London:Virago, 1986 edn.)

'Introduction', in Dorothy Edwards, *Rhapsody* (London:Virago, 1986 edn.)

'Introduction', in F. Tennyson Jesse, *A Pin to See the Peepshow* (London:Virago, 1979 edn).

'Darwin and Feminism', *Collegium Anthropologicum*, 6 January 1992.

D: UNPUBLISHED WRITING

'Twm Shon Catti' – unpublished play commissioned by the Welsh Drama Company's Schools Theatre Programme, 1973.

'What's Got Into You?', unpublished play commissioned by Bag and Baggage Theatre Company (Cardiff), 1980.

E: TRANSLATIONS OF WORKS

Teli'r Teulu: Comedi Dair Act (Aberystwyth: Gwasg Aberystwyth, 1960)

Droit de Meutre (Paris, 1969)

The Descent of Woman

De Vrouw, Onze Voorvader (Amsterdam: Elsevier, 1972)

L'Origine Della Donna (Turin: Einaudi, 1972)

Der Mythos vom schwachen Gerschlechten:Wie die Frauen wurden was sie sind (Dusseldorf: Econ Verlag, 1972)

La Fin du Surmale (Paris: Calmann-Levy, 1973)

Hvor Korn Kvinden Fra? (Copenhagen, Gyldendal, 1973)

Naisen Esihistoria (Helsinki: Otava, 1973)

Eva al Desnudo (Barcelona: Pomaire, 1973)

Porijeklo Zene (Zagreb: August Cesarec, 1978)

Kvinnans Nedkomst (Stockholm: Forum, 1978)

Falling Apart

La Cuidad en Crisis (Barcelona: Pomaire, 1979)

Stad in Stukken (Bussum: Agathon, 1980)

The Aquatic Ape

Vattenapan (Stockholm: Forum, 1983)

Des Origines Aquatiques de l'homme (Paris: Editions Sand, 1988)

Kinder des Ozeans (Munich: Goldmann, 1988)

The Scars of Evolution
Evoluution Arvet (Helsinki: Kirjayhtyma, 1992)
Udviklingens Pris (Copenhagen: Gyldenhal, 1993)
Les cicatrices de l'evolution (Chiroulet: Gaia, 1994)
Sporen van de Evolutie (Baarn: Ambo, 1996)

PART 2: BROADCASTING

Title	Programme/Series	Network	Channel	Broadcast date
Let's Do an Experiment	Woman's Hour	BBC	Light Programme	26 October 1950
My Embarrassing Half Hour	Woman's Hour	BBC	Light Programme	24 April 1951
The Thing	Woman's Hour	BBC	Light Programme	18 December 1951
Rose Around the Door	Woman's Hour	BBC	Light Programme	11 March 1952
Home on the Range	For the Schools/ Let's Join In	BBC	Home Service	16 June 1952
Baker	Woman's Hour	BBC	Light Programme	21 April 1953
Concert	Woman's Hour	BBC	Light Programme	5 February 1954
Reprieve?		BBC	Home Service (Welsh)	10 August 1954
Question Time	Younger Generation	BBC	Light Programme	3 March 1955
Mirror, Mirror		BBC	TV	20 March 1955
The Tamer Tamed		BBC	Home Service (Welsh)	4 October 1955
Wilde West		BBC	TV	8 December 1955
The Tamer Tamed		BBC	TV	7 February 1956
	What Do You Know?	BBC	Light Programme	30 April 1956
Welsh Housewife		BBC	North American Service	29 May 1956
Without Vision		BBC	TV	10 July 1956
	Welsh Magazine	BBC	Overseas Service	23 July 1956
	Welsh Magazine	BBC	Overseas Service	4 September 1956
	Welsh Magazine	BBC	Overseas Service	16 October 1956
	Welsh Magazine	BBC	Overseas Service	27 November 1956
F.S.U.		BBC	TV	3 January 1957
Eleven Plus		BBC	TV	22 January 1957
	Commonwealth Roundup	BBC	North American Service	5 April 1957
	Welsh Magazine	BBC	Overseas Service	9 May 1957
Do It Yourself		BBC	TV	26 May 1957
	Welsh Magazine	BBC	Overseas Service	4 June 1957
Cuckoo		BBC	TV	1 September 1957
	Welsh Magazine	BBC	Overseas Service	6 September 1957
	Welsh Magazine	BBC	Overseas Service	24 September 1957
	Welsh Magazine	BBC	Overseas Service	4 December 1957
Black Furrow		BBC	TV	4 March 1958
	Welsh Magazine	BBC	Overseas Service	6 March 1958
	Welsh Bookshelf	BBC	Home Service (Welsh)	11 March 1958
	Welsh Magazine	BBC	Overseas Service	13 March 1958
You're A Long Time Dead		BBC	TV	13 February 1958
	Newspoint	BBC	Home Service (Welsh)	15 April 1958

Title	Programme/Series	Network	Channel	Broadcast date
The Waiting Room		BBC	TV	6 May 1958
Every Minute Counts	Encounter	CBC (Canada)		27 May 1958
	Ask Me Another	BBC	TV	21 July 1958
	Mirror	BBC	Home Service (Welsh)	12 September 1958
Rest You Merry		BBC	TV	17 December 1958
	Hook-Up	BBC		Home Service
(Welsh)				31 March 1959
	Welsh Magazine	BBC	Overseas Service	3 June 1959
	Hook-Up	BBC	Home Service (Welsh)	15 July 1959
Mary Hughes of Mayfair and Stepney	Two of A Kind	BBC	Home Service	8 March 1960
The Conspiracy	Inside Story	ITV	TV	13 March 1960
Part 1	A Matter of Degree	BBC	TV	16 May 1960
Part 2	A Matter of Degree	BBC	TV	23 May 1960
	Trans Canada Magazine	BBC	North American Service	26 May 1960
Part 3	A Matter of Degree	BBC	TV	30 May 1960
Part 4	A Matter of Degree	BBC	TV	6 June 1960
Part 5	A Matter of Degree	BBC	TV	13 June 1960
Part 6	A Matter of Degree	BBC	TV	20 June 1960
Looking for Garrow	Sunday Night Play	BBC	TV	30 October 1960
	Voice of the Artist	BBC	Home Service (Welsh)	11 November 1960
The Soldier and the Woman		BBC	TV	29 December 1960
Fury in Petticoats		BBC	TV	26 March 1961
Blackout		BBC	Home Service (Welsh)	30 March 1961
	Women's Programme	BBC	North American Service	30 April 1961
	Home Make Competition	BBC	TV	11 May 1961
	Woman's Hour	BBC	Light Programme	23 May 1961
Strictly Confidential		BBC	Light Programme	3 November 1961
	In Wales Today	BBC	TV	21 December 1961
Episode One	Barbara in Black	BBC	TV	19 February 1962
Episode Two	Barbara in Black	BBC	TV	26 February 1962
Episode Three	Barbara in Black	BBC	TV	5 March 1962
Episode Four	Barbara in Black	BBC	TV	12 March 1962
Episode Five	Barbara in Black	BBC	TV	19 March 1962
Episode Six	Barbara in Black	BBC	TV	26 March 1962
	Women's Programme	BBC	North American Service	9 April 1962
A Chance to Shine		BBC	TV	2 November 1962
The Canterville Ghost	Sunday Night Play	BBC	TV	23 December 1962
	Tonight	BBC	TV	26 March 1963
Part 1	Epitaph for a Spy	BBC	TV	19 May 1963
Part 2	Epitaph for a Spy	BBC	TV	26 May 1963
Part 3	Epitaph for a Spy	BBC	TV	2 June 1963
Part 4	Epitaph for a Spy	BBC	TV	9 June 1963
Can't You Drive a Little Faster?	Taxi!	BBC	TV	21 September 1963
The Rescuers	Encore	BBC	TV	23 September 1963

Title	Programme/Series	Network	Channel	Broadcast Date
The Fontenay Murders	Maigret	BBC	TV	8 October 1963
The Face Saver	Dr Finlay's Casebook	BBC	TV	8 November 1963
The Log of the Cap Fagnet	Maigret	BBC	TV	19 November 1963
The Judge's House	Maigret	BBC	TV	26 November 1963
The Soldier and the Woman	Afternoon Theatre	BBC	Home Service	18 December 1963
Fury in Petticoats	Afternoon Theatre	BBC	Home Service	5 February 1964
A Change to Shine	Mid-Week Theatre	BBC	Light Programme	11 March 1964
Ideas in the Air	Woman's Hour	BBC	Light Programme	15 May 1964
Fire	Mary Barton	BBC	Two	20 June 1964
Violence	Mary Barton	BBC	Two	27 June 1964
Murder	Mary Barton	BBC	Two	4 July 1964
Trial	Mary Barton	BBC	Two	11 July 1964
Thunderbolt	R.3 Ministry of Research Centre No. 3	BBC	One	18 December 1964
In Committee	Dr Finlay's Casebook	BBC	One	18 April 1965
The Sultan	Lil (Series One)	BBC	One (Wales)	23 April 1965
A Little Lovelier	Lil (Series One)	BBC	One (Wales)	30 April 1965
The Surgery	Lil (Series One)	BBC	One (Wales)	7 May 1965
Chapter and Verse	Lil (Series One)	BBC	One (Wales)	14 May 1965
Will You Be Mine?	Lil (Series One)	BBC	One (Wales)	21 May 1965
A Patch of Damp	Lil (Series One)	BBC	One (Wales)	28 May 1865
A Woman's Work	Dr Finlay's Casebook	BBC	One (Wales)	13 June 1965
The Waiting Room		BBC	Light Programme	9 August 1965
The Longest Visit	Dr Finlay's Casebook	BBC	One	12 December 1965
And the Lonely Hearts	Lil (Series Two)	BBC	One (Wales)	24 December 1965
The Boycott	Lil (Series Two)	BBC	One (Wales)	7 January 1966
The Chair	Lil (Series Two)	BBC	One (Wales)	14 January 1966
Look After Pinkie	Lil (Series Two)	BBC	One (Wales)	21 January 1966
The Tea Break	Lil (Series Two)	BBC	One (Wales)	28 January 1966
I'm in Charge	Lil (Series Two)	BBC	One (Wales)	4 February 1966
The Celebrity	Lil (Series Two)	BBC	One (Wales)	11 February 1966
A Matter of People	Home This Afternoon	BBC	Home Service	15 April 1966
Crusade	Dr Finlay's Casebook	BBC	One	24 April 1966
The Legacy	Dr Finlay's Casebook	BBC	One	1 May 1966
What shall we do with the drunken sailor?	King of the River	BBC	One	27 July 1966
Aboard the Lugger	King of the River	BBC	One	24 August 1966
Why Me?	Out of Town Theatre	BBC	One	18 November 1966
	Talking Shop	BBc	Home Service (Welsh)	10 March 1967
Keep him till I come home for him	Sanctuary	ITV		3 July 1967
	Week In, Week Out	BBC	One	4 August 1967
Accidents Never Happen	Dr Finlay's Casebook	BBC	One	6 November 1967
	Rhwng Sir a Sir - Glamorganshire	BBC	Wales	3 March 1968
Conscience Clause	Dr Finlay's Casebook	BBC	One	21 January 1968
Never Get Involved	Sanctuary	ITV		8 April 1968

Title	Programme/Series	Network	Channel	Broadcast Date
	Crosstalk	BBC	One	23 April 1968
	Crosstalk	BBC	One	10 May 1968
	Crosstalk	BBC	One	14 May 1968
	Crosstalk	BBC	One	17 May 1968
	Crosstalk	BBC	One	24 May 1968
Zombie	Television Theatre	BBC	One	22 July 1968
	Crosstalk	BBC	One	25 July 1968
Episode One	One of the Family (Series One)	BBC	Wales	13 September 1968
Episode Two	One of the Family (Series One)	BBC	Wales	20 September 1968
	Crosstalk	BBC	One	10 October 1968
Episode Five	One of the Family (Series One)	BBC	Wales	11 October 1968
Episode Six	One of the Family (Series One)	BBC	Wales	18 October 1968
Episode Nine	One of the Family (Series One)	BBC	Wales	8 November 1968
Episode Ten	One of the Family (Series One)	BBC	Wales	15 November 1968
Episode Fourteen	One of the Family (Series One)	BBC	Wales	13 December 1968
Episode Fifteen	One of the Family (Series One)	BBC	Wales	20 December 1968
	Dysgu Cymraeg	BBC	Wales	22 January 1969
	Dysgu Cymraeg	BBC	Wales	5 February 1969
	Dysgu Cymraeg	BBC	Wales	19 February 1969
	Dysgu Cymraeg	BBC	Wales	5 March 1969
	Dysgu Cymraeg	BBC	Wales	19 March 1969
	Dysgu Cymraeg	BBC	Wales	23 April 1969
Big Ben	Dr Finlay's Casebook	BBC	One	27 April 1969
	Dysgu Cymraeg	BBC	Wales	7 May 1969
	Dysgu Cymraeg	BBC	Wales	21 May 1969
	Dysgu Cymraeg	BBC	Wales	11 June 1969
Episode Three	One of the Family (Series Two)	BBC	Wales	7 October 1969
Episode Four	One of the Family (Series Two)	BBC	Wales	14 October 1969
Episode Seven	One of the Family (Series Two)	BBC	Wales	4 November 1969
Episode Eight	One of the Family (Series Two)	BBC	Wales	11 November 1969
	The Doctors	BBC	One	26 November 1969
	The Doctors	BBC	One	27 November 1969
Episode Eleven	One of the Family (Series Two)	BBC	Wales	2 December 1969
Episode Twelve	One of the Family (Series Two)	BBC	Wales	9 December 1969
	The Doctors	BBC	One	17 December 1969
	The Doctors	BBC	One	18 December 1969
	The Doctors	BBC	One	7 January 1970
	The Doctors	BBC	One	8 January 1970
	The Doctors	BBC	One	25 February 1970
	The Doctors	BBC	One	26 February 1970
	The Doctors	BBC	One	25 March 1970
	The Doctors	BBC	One	26 March 1970
	The Doctors	BBC	One	6 May 1970
	The Doctors	BBC	One	7 May 1970
If It's Got Your Number On It		ITV		28 July 1970
	The Doctors	BBC	One	26 August 1970
	The Doctors	BBC	One	27 August 1970

Title	Programme/Series	Network	Channel	Broadcast Date
	The Doctors	BBC	One	23 September 1970
	The Doctors	BBC	One	24 September 1970
	The Doctors	BBC	One	21 October 1970
	The Doctors	BBC	One	22 October 1970
	The Doctors	BBC	One	2 December 1970
	The Doctors	BBC	One	3 December 1970
Dust	Dr Finlay's Casebook	BBC	One	13 December 1970
The Soldier and the Woman	Afternoon Theatre	BBC	Radio 4	18 December 1970
	The Doctors	BBC	One	20 January 1971
	The Doctors	BBC	One	21 January 1971
	The Doctors	BBC	One	10 March 1971
	The Doctors	BBC	One	11 March 1971
	The Doctors	BBC	One	12 May 1971
	The Doctors	BBC	One	13 May 1971
	The Doctors	BBC	One	9 June 1971
	The Doctors	BBC	One	10 June 1971
You're A Long Time Dead	Saturday Night Theatre	BBC	Radio 4	28 August 1971
Do We Owe the Artist a Living?	Woman's Hour	BBC	Radio 2	18 February 1972
Talking Point	Woman's Hour	BBC	Radio 2	5 May 1972
A Woman Alone	The Onedin Line	BBC	One	1 October 1972
The Descent of Woman		BBC	Radio 4	10 October 1972
Come On In, The Water's Lovely		BBC	Two	19 October 1972
	Woman's Hour	BBC	Radio 2	20 October 1972
	Questions of Belief	BBC	Radio 4	22 October 1972
Liberation Now		BBC	One	1 December 1972
Crusade	Dr Finlay's Casebook	BBC	Radio 4	11 December 1972
	No Man's Land	ITV		10 February 1973
	A Word in Edgeways	BBC	Radio 4	17 March 1973
Part One	A Pin to See the Peepshow	BBC	Two	26 July 1973
Part Two	A Pin to See the Peepshow	BBC	Two	2 August 1973
Part Three	A Pin to See the Peepshow	BBC	Two	9 August 1973
Part Four	A Pin to See the Peepshow	BBC	Two	16 August 1973
Come into my Parlour	Orson Welles' Great Mysteries	ITV		26 January 1974
Possessions		ITV		26 May 1974
Accidents Never Happen	Dr Finlay's Casebook	BBC	Radio 4	12 November 1974
Joey	Horizon	BBC	Two	9 December 1974
The Face Saver	Dr Finlay's Casebook	BBC	Radio 4	7 January 1975
Part One	Anne of Avonlea	BBC	One	26 January 1975
Part Two	Anne of Avonlea	BBC	One	1 February 1975
Part Three	Anne of Avonlea	BBC	One	8 February 1975
Part Four	Anne of Avonlea	BBC	One	16 February 1975
Part Five	Anne of Avonlea	BBC	One	23 February 1975
Part Six	Anne of Avonlea	BBC	One	1 March 1975
	Any Questions?	BBC	Radio 4	5 April 1975
In the Public Interest	General Hospital	ITV		25 July 1975
First Day	Rape of the Fair Country	BBC	Radio 4	3 August 1975

Title	Programme/Series	Network	Channel	Broadcast Date
First Love	Rape of the Fair Country	BBC	Radio 4	10 August 1975
The Mark of the Scab	Rape of the Fair Country	BBC	Radio 4	17 August 1975
March to Freedom	Rape of the Fair Country	BBC	Radio 4	24 August 1975
Part One	How Green Was My Valley	BBC	Two	29 December 1975
Part Two	How Green Was My Valley	BBC	Two	5 January 1976
Part Three	How Green Was My Valley	BBC	Two	12 January 1976
Part Four	How Green Was My Valley	BBC	Two	19 January 1976
Part Five	How Green Was My Valley	BBC	Two	26 January 1976
Part Six	How Green Was My Valley	BBC	Two	2 February 1976
Arrivals and Departures	Brothers	BBC	One	10 October 1976
The Distaff Side	Brothers	BBC	One	17 October 1976
Cross Currents	Brothers	BBC	One	24 October 1976
Falling Apart	Woman's Hour	BBC	Radio 4	10 December 1976
	The Better Half	BBC	Radio 4	28 February 1977
	Woman's Hour	BBC	Radio 4	13 April 1977
In Defence of Virgins		BBC	Radio 4	20 July 1977
Part One: 1886	Marie Curie	BBC	Two	16 August 1977
	Pandora's Box	ITV		20 August 1977
Part Two: 1895	Marie Curie	BBC	Two	23 August 1977
Part Three: 1898	Marie Curie	BBC	Two	30 August 1977
Part Four: 1904	Marie Curie	BBC	Two	6 September 1977
Part Five: 1911	Marie Curie	BBC	Two	13 September 1977
My Delight		BBC	Radio 4	9 September 1977
A Christmas Carol		BBC	Two	24 December 1977
Glenys	A Woman's Place	BBC	Two	9 May 1978
Jean	A Woman's Place	BBC	Two	23 May 1978
	Off to Philadelphia in the Morning	BBC	One	12 September 1978
	Off to Philadelphia in the Morning	BBC	One	19 September 1978
	Off to Philadelphia in the Morning	BBC	One	26 September 1978
Wednesday's Child		BBC	Two	1 November 1979
Part One: Buxton, 1913	Testament of Youth	BBC	Two	4 November 1979
Part Two: Buxton, 1914	Testament of Youth	BBC	Two	11 November 1979
Part Three: 1915	Testament of Youth	BBC	Two	18 November 1979
Part Four: 1917	Testament of Youth	BBC	Two	25 November 1979
Part Five: 1918	Testament of Youth	BBC	Two	2 December 1979
Review of Dear Old Blighty	Kaleidoscope	BBC	Radio 4	5 February 1980
Review of The Diary of a Farmer's Wife	Kaleidoscope	BBC	Radio 4	28 May 1980
Don't Try, Do It	The Life and Times of David Lloyd George	BBC	Two	4 March 1981
A Wicked War	The Life and Times of David Lloyd George	BBC	Two	11 March 1981
He is Wise, and Merciful	The Life and Times of David Lloyd George	BBC	Two	18 March 1981
All Flesh is Grass	The Life and Times of David Lloyd George	BBC	Two	25 March 1981

Title	Programme/Series	Network	Channel	Broadcast Date
Well, We're In	The Life and Times of David Lloyd George	BBC	Two	1 April 1981
No. 10	The Life and Times of David Lloyd George	BBC	Two	8 April 1981
Review of The Mabinogi	Kaleidoscope	BBC	Radio 4	13 April 1981
An Honourable Peace	The Life and Times of David Lloyd George	BBC	Two	15 April 1981
Win or Lose	The Life and Times of David Lloyd George	BBC	Two	22 April 1981
	Who Do I Think I Am?	BBC	Radio 4	28 April 1981
Footnotes of History	The Life and Times of David Lloyd George	BBC	Two	29 April 1981
	Did You See...?	BBC	Two	28 November 1981
Part One	Fame is the Spur	BBC	Two	8 January 1982
Part Two	Fame is the Spur	BBC	Two	15 January 1982
Part Three	Fame is the Spur	BBC	Two	22 January 1982
Part Four	Fame is the Spur	BBC	Two	29 January 1982
Part Five	Fame is the Spur	BBC	Two	5 February 1982
For the Love of Egypt	Chronicle Over Egypt	BBC	Two	10 February 1982
Part Six	Fame is the Spur	BBC	Two	12 February 1982
Part Seven	Fame is the Spur	BBC	Two	19 February 1982
Part Eight	Fame is the Spur	BBC	Two	26 February 1982
The Fontenay Murders	Maigret	BBC	One	21 November 1982
	Milestones	BBC	Radio Wales	13 December 1982
The Forgotten Voyage		BBC	Two	24 December 1982
	Did You See...?	BBC	Two	4 March 1983
	Quote... Unquote	BBC	Radio 4	16 July 1983
	Good Books	BBC	World Service	23 July 1983
	Quote... Unquote	BBC	Radio 4	22 August 1983
	Quote... Unquote	BBC	Radio 4	26 December 1983
The Garden of Inheritance	The Natural World	BBC	Two	6 February 1984
	Did You See...?	BBC	Two	12 February 1984
	Did You See...?	BBC	Two	4 March 1984
Journey into the Shadows		BBC	Two	27 May 1984
	Rollercoaster	BBC	Radio 4	12 July 1984
	Quote... Unquote	BBC	Radio 4	27 December 1984
What's Got Into You?	The Afternoon Play	BBC	Radio 4	15 January 1985
The Burston Rebellion	Screen Two	BBC	Two	24 February 1985
	The Diary of Anne Frank	BBC	One	4 January 1987
	The Diary of Anne Frank	BBC	One	11 January 1987
	The Diary of Anne Frank	BBC	One	18 January 1987
	The Diary of Anne Frank	BBC	One	25 January 1987
Sputnik, Bleeps and Mr Perry		Channel 4		25 March 1987
Downstarts	The Afternoon Play	BBC	Radio 4	8 October 1987
Stanley	Screen Two	BBC	Two	31 January 1988
Death of a Ghost: Part One	Campion	BBC	One	5 March 1989
Death of a Ghost: Part Two	Campion	BBC	One	12 March 1989
The Anthropologist	Woman's Hour	BBC	Radio 4	2 November 1990

INDEX

The index covers the main text only; the endnotes have not been indexed. Entries for towns or villages denote significant events in those locations; scattered references to each location have not been included. Details of Elaine Morgan's life have been indexed thematically as a guide for readers and have been restricted primarily to screenwriting, publications, public activities, and selected views on matters of interest.

AUTHOR NOTE

Daryl Leeworthy is a writer and historian. He is the Rhys Davies Research Fellow at the South Wales Miners' Library at Swansea University, where he continues to research the historical experience of the South Wales Coalfield. He was educated in Pontypridd and read history and politics at Oriel College, Oxford. Following postgraduate studies in Canada, he completed his doctoral research at Swansea University in 2011.

He has taught at several universities across Britain, including the University of Huddersfield (where he was lecturer in community history), the Open University, Cardiff University, and Swansea University, and has been active as a tutor in community-based adult learning for many years delivering classes across the South Wales Valleys. He is currently a member of the governing body of Addysg Oedolion Cymru | Adult Learning Wales.

His many publications on the history and literature of Wales include *Labour Country: Political Radicalism and Social Democracy in South Wales, 1831-1985* (2018) and *A Little Gay History of Wales* (2019).